GOOD HOUSEKEEPING
MIXER
COOKBOOK

GOOD HOUSEKEEPING
MIXER
COOKBOOK

by
Good Housekeeping
Institute

EBURY PRESS
LONDON

Published by Ebury Press
National Magazine House
72 Broadwick Street
London W1V 2BP

First impression 1980

ISBN 0 85223 172 5

Editor Patricia Mackinnon
Home economist Susanna Tee
Designer Derek Morrison
Colour photography by Melvin Grey
Jacket design by Harry Green
and photograph by Roger Tuff
Line drawings by Pat Robson

Jacket illustration shows:
Sausage and bacon savoury en croûte (page 36),
Carrot cake (page 98), Mushroom mustard burgers (page 42),
Iced cucumber mint soup (page 31), Venetian creams (page 87),
Beef and walnut pie (page 43)

Food processor kindly loaned by ICTC

Printed in Great Britain at the
University Press, Cambridge

Contents

How to Use this Book

INTRODUCTION

In order to exploit your machine to the full, whether it be a food processor, mixer or blender, it is essential to know exactly what it will do. Read the introduction carefully (pages 10–21) and follow the directions in the instruction manual.

SYMBOLS

We have used symbols to indicate which types of mixer would be useful in the preparation of each recipe, as follows:

⊛ Food processor

▼ Blender

♦ Mixer

♦+ Mixer plus attachments (mincer, slicer and shredder)

Every recipe has been included because it can be made more quickly or easily with the help of one, or sometimes more than one, machine but this does *not* mean that you have to own every type of mixer indicated in order to prepare a recipe.

Take Salad ham ring ⊛ ▼ ♦+ on page 27, for example:
a food processor would be useful for shredding the lettuce and mincing the ham and onion, but this could also be done with a mixer and the appropriate attachments, and either a food processor or a blender could be used to purée the lettuce.

Some recipes are geared to particular machines (you might not want to chop pounds of onions without the help of a food processor or purée large quantities without a blender) but some of the machines indicated have a more marginal use. For example, for Brown bread ice cream ⊛ ▼ ♦ on page 82:
the food processor and blender would be useful only for making the breadcrumbs; what you really need for this recipe is the mixer.

So use the symbols as a guideline, reading through recipes before you begin to cook and deciding just how much of the preparation can be done with the help of your particular mixer.

INGREDIENTS

In recipes using raw minced meat we have suggested in the ingredients that the meat be bought in a piece rather than already minced, assuming that owners of food processors or mixers with mincing attachments will prefer to do their own mincing at home. If you have no mincing machine, simply substitute the same amount of butcher's minced meat.

COOKERY TECHNIQUES

Here is a summary of what everyday instructions mean in terms of a mixer. See the introduction (pages 10–21) for more details.

Beat   Use your table or hand mixer or a food processor instead of a wooden spoon to beat air into batters or cake mixtures.

Blend   When we say blend, we mean use a blender or food processor to turn ingredients into a purée (except for blending very small amounts of flour or cornflour to a paste with a little cold water).

Chop   For hard vegetables like onions you need a food processor, or for small amounts, one of the more powerful blenders.

Cream   Use a table or hand mixer or a food processor instead of a wooden spoon to cream fat and sugar together.

Grate/ Slice   The slicer/shredder attachment on a table mixer or the slicing/shredding discs of a food processor are invaluable for coping with large quantities.

Mince   Raw or cooked meat and some vegetables can be minced using the attachment for a table mixer or a food processor.

Mix   A table or hand mixer or a food processor can be used to combine fat with flour for pastry, scones and cakes. So in this book you won't find any instructions to rub in.

Whip   Use your table or hand mixer to whip cream.

Whisk   Egg whites can be whisked with a hand or table mixer.

Handy Cookery Charts

CONVERSION TO METRIC MEASUREMENTS

The metric measures in this book are based on a 25 g unit instead of the ounce (28.35 g). Slight adjustments to this basic conversion standard were necessary in some recipes to achieve satisfactory cooking results.

If you want to convert your own recipes from imperial to metric, we suggest you use the same 25 g unit, and use 600 ml in place of 1 pint, with the British Standard 5-ml and 15-ml spoons replacing the old variable teaspoons and tablespoons; these adaptations will sometimes give a slightly smaller recipe quantity and may require a shorter cooking time.

Note Sets of British Standard metric measuring spoons are available in the following sizes – 2.5 ml, 5 ml, 10 ml and 15 ml.

When measuring milk it is more convenient to the exact conversion of 568 ml (1 pint).

For more general reference, the following tables will be helpful.

METRIC CONVERSION SCALE

Liquid				Solid		
Imperial	*Exact conversion*	*Recommended ml*		*Imperial*	*Exact conversion*	*Recommended g*
$\frac{1}{4}$ pint	142 ml	150 ml		1 oz	28.35 g	25 g
$\frac{1}{2}$ pint	284 ml	300 ml		2 oz	56.7 g	50 g
1 pint	568 ml	600 ml		4 oz	113.4 g	100 g
$1\frac{1}{2}$ pints	851 ml	900 ml		8 oz	226.8 g	225 g
$1\frac{3}{4}$ pints	992 ml	1 litre		12 oz	340.2 g	325 g
For quantities of $1\frac{3}{4}$ pints and over, litres and fractions of a litre have been used.				14 oz	397.0 g	400 g
				16 oz (1 lb)	453.6 g	450 g
				1 kilogram (kg) equals 2.2 lb		

Follow either the metric or the imperial measures in the recipes as they are not interchangeable.

OVEN TEMPERATURE CHART

°C	°F	Gas mark		°C	°F	Gas mark
120	225	$\frac{1}{4}$		190	375	5
130	250	$\frac{1}{2}$		200	400	6
140	275	1		220	425	7
150	300	2		230	450	8
170	325	3		240	475	9
180	350	4				

Note Where a recipe requires 175 g (6 oz) shortcrust pastry, use 100 g (4 oz) flour, following the recipe on page 57.

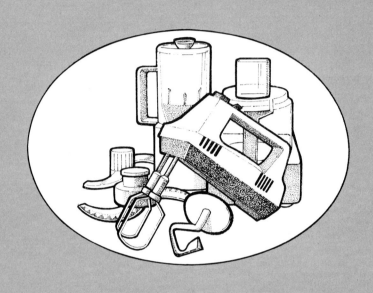

Introduction

There is no doubt that a multitude of food preparation jobs can be speeded up by the use of an electric mixer, food processor or blender. They make light work of chopping, shredding, slicing, mincing or grating and take the toil out of mixing, blending, whisking, beating or creaming. But the term 'mixer' covers a wide and perhaps confusing range of types and models, each designed for slightly different cooking needs. Here is a guide to the types of mixers, blenders and food processors available, as well as advice on how to get the most out of the one you have chosen.

Mixers fall into four main groups. Table mixers and food processors are essentially for family cooking or for bulk cooking for the freezer. Hand mixers are less versatile, but easy to use and store and efficient within their capabilities. They are also less expensive. Blenders, sometimes called liquidizers, are rather more specific in their use and can be bought either as attachments to table and hand mixers or as independent units.

To get the most out of your mixer it is essential to know its capabilities and how to use it properly. The second part of the introduction (page 16) covers such essentials as assembling the machines and running the motors at the correct speeds and goes on to give specific advice on mixing various ingredients. Cleaning instructions and safety rules complete the section. Once you have mastered the techniques you will be able to purée vegetables and fruits for soups and desserts in a matter of seconds, mix bread doughs, cakes and pastry with the least possible effort or chop raw vegetables, nuts or meat in no time at all.

Types of mixer and what they will do

Table Mixers

These are large, fairly heavy machines which are particularly good for mixing ingredients for baking or for such tasks as whipping cream or making mayonnaise. Generally they are not designed to cope with very small quantities – a two-egg sandwich cake is about the smallest practical size to mix in them. They will, however, mix large and heavy quantities efficiently – for example, rich fruit cakes up to sixteen-egg size and bread dough for four loaves. To change from cake making to whisking to dough kneading usually entails a simple change of beater, but to do anything but the basic creaming, beating and whisking jobs attachments are necessary (see opposite).

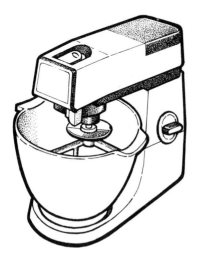

A typical table mixer

Different designs

There are two basic designs of table mixer; the traditional type with a motor arm to operate the beaters within a bowl on the base of the stand, and the case type which has the motor housed in a neat casing. In the casing there are two drive outlets – a high speed one for attachments like the blender and a normal speed one for the bowl and beaters. This second type is a little more compact than the traditional mixer but not usually as powerful. There is also a variation on the case type, where the motor is fixed under the work surface and holes are cut for the connecting spindles so that the bowl and beaters and the various attachments can be slotted into place when required. This can also be a very neat and compact arrangement which leaves the work space free when the mixer is not in use, but of course room has to be allowed for the storage of the bowl and all the attachments.

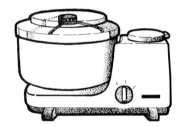

A table mixer with the motor housed in a casing

Attachments

Table mixers are available with a wide range of attachments:

dough hook, blender (liquidizer), coffee grinder, juice separator, mincer, slicer and shredder, juice extractor, cream maker, can opener, colander and sieve, potato peeler, bean and peel slicer, wheat mill, sausage filler.

Not all of these are available with every make of mixer. Before buying, be sure you will use each attachment enough to make its purchase worthwhile. The most important, for many households, are the blender (liquidizer), slicer/shredder and mincer.

The blending goblet purées fresh and cooked fruit and vegetables, crumbs fresh bread and does many other jobs (see page 15), while the slicer/shredder slices fruit and vegetables and grates such foods as nuts and chocolate. The mincer is particularly useful for preparing raw and cooked meat for a huge range of recipes. Other attachments might also be of particular use: the bean and peel slicer for runner beans and marmalade, juice extractor for citrus fruits, juice separator for getting the juice out of vegetables and fruits, and perhaps an attachment for stuffing sausages and a wheat mill for making your own flour. These attachments are all rather bulky to store. They also have to be fitted onto the machine which can be a fiddly job, but for large quantities it is worth the effort of getting them out of the cupboard and putting them into position on the mixer.

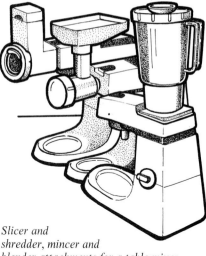

Slicer and shredder, mincer and blender attachments for a table mixer

13

Table mixers have to be used with the bowl supplied and you have to take the food to be mixed or prepared to the mixer (hand mixers, see opposite, can be used in any bowl). Some people find it difficult to add food to the blender attachment, which has to be fixed on top of the motor arm, thus raising the top to about 45–60 cm (18–24 inches) above the work surface. Table mixers are, however, easy to use, efficient (especially for bulk cooking), robust and simple to clean.

Food Processors

These versatile machines are more compact and lighter than table mixers. They are good for preparing family meals and for bulk cooking. Although they cannot mix such large quantities at one time as table mixers, they operate at such speed that it is no trouble to process two or three batches one after the other. Food processors are easy to use and clean and once you are used to the techniques they save a lot of food preparation time.

Different designs

Food processors usually consist of a motor housing unit with a bowl which fits on to the central spindle on the stand, a lid with a feed tube in it and a food pusher. Most of them have a selection of stainless steel cutters – a double knife blade for chopping, blending and mixing and discs for slicing and shredding to various sizes. The number of discs and cutters varies with different models. Some, for example, have a plastic cutter for soft mixtures like creamed cakes and mashed potatoes and for kneading doughs. Others, usually known as food preparation machines, are a little more complicated. They have a motor housing on which is fixed a chopping unit, a mixing bowl unit, a blender goblet or a vegetable chef attachment. Most food processors work at one or two speeds, though some have a 'burst' position which turns the motor on or off to work in short sharp bursts instead of continuously.

Blending, in most machines, is done in the bowl using the double knife. With the same knife, also in the bowl, raw or cooked meat is minced in seconds. Hard foods for chopping or slicing, or liquids, are fed into the bowl through the feed tube, using the pusher to press vegetables onto the slicing or shredding disc when necessary. The knives and cutters are quick and easy to change and the fact that you can carry out many food preparation jobs using the same bowl, with a simple change of disc or knife, greatly speeds up your cooking.

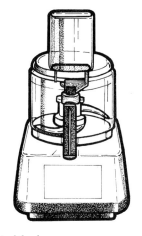

A typical food processor

Slicing and grating discs and chopping and mixing blades for a food processor

14

Food processors are not on the whole as efficient for cake making, whipping cream and whisking egg whites as table mixers. The action and design of the fast moving knife blades do not incorporate as much air into any mixture as the traditional beaters and whisks of a table mixer, and cakes tend to have a closer texture. Some models have a round, tilted bowl. These give better textured cakes and can be used satisfactorily for egg whites and cream. Slightly different cake making techniques, for example using rubbed-in rather than creamed mixtures, also help towards more satisfactory baking.

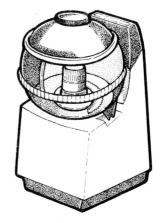

Models with a tilted bowl are better for cream or egg whites

Hand Mixers

As the name implies, these are usually hand held and can be used to mix, whisk or beat ingredients, in any suitably sized bowl or saucepan. They can be used for mashing potatoes in a saucepan or for whisking a basic fatless sponge in a bowl over a saucepan of hot water on the stove.

Different designs

Many hand mixers are available with a stand and bowl, when they operate like a table mixer except that they are less powerful and will not cope with large quantities and heavy mixtures. However these models certainly mix small quantities very well. Many people do not bother to buy the stand and bowl, perhaps because they realize that the main advantage of a hand mixer lies in the fact that it can be taken to any pan or bowl you are using for mixing. For some, however, the stand is worthwhile, and so too are the attachments for blending (liquidizing) and for slicing and shredding. Some models also have a coffee mill available with them which as well as grinding coffee beans is also useful for chopping nuts and grinding spices. Hand mixers normally operate at three different speeds. Without a stand they can be kept ready for use on a neat wall bracket.

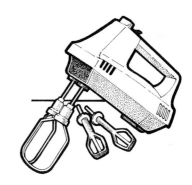

A hand held mixer

Blenders (liquidizers)

These goblet shaped mixers do the same food preparation jobs as the blending attachments on table mixers or the chopping knives in the bowl of a food processor. Their capacity is a little greater than that of the optional blending attachment for a hand mixer. Their prime use is for making purées, blending liquid ingredients, blending liquid and fine ingredients like flour, making breadcrumbs and chopping small quantities of raw fruit and vegetables, but they can also be

Some hand mixers have stands and attachments

15

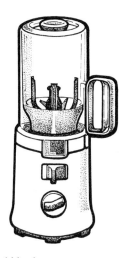

A typical blender

used for batters and cake mixtures (special recipes are needed). The more you use a blender the more uses you find for one – mayonnaise, pâtés and innumerable light, fluffy desserts can be produced with minimum effort.

Different designs

Independent models have an advantage over those designed as attachments to table or hand mixers because they stand firmly on the work top and are always ready for use. Blenders may have only one speed or as many as seven, and some have an additional 'burst' position (see page 14). A two or three-speed model is usually satisfactory for most jobs. The goblet may be of plastic or toughened glass. Some of the plastic ones will not withstand boiling liquids or washing in a machine. It is convenient if the goblet is calibrated in millilitres and fluid ounces and also if it has a handle to facilitate pouring. Another asset is a removable stopper or bung in the lid which enables small amounts of food or liquid to be added to the mixture in the goblet when the motor is switched on, for example when adding the oil to a mayonnaise mixture. A more sophisticated development is the blender with a built-in heater, which makes it possible to blend raw ingredients for soup, for example, then leave the goblet in position with the heater switch turned on to cook the mixture. Some independent blenders have a coffee grinding attachment.

Getting the most out of your mixer

Whatever type of mixer, blender or food processor you have, you will get more use out of it if it is kept on the work surface ready for action rather than tucked away in a cupboard. The manufacturer's instruction booklet or leaflet will give you exact details of what your particular machine will do, and on the best way of looking after it: keep it handy for reference. There are, however, some general rules for making best use of your mixer, regardless of the model you own, and they give useful guidelines on the basic running of the machines, on the way to get first-class results with a variety of recipes and on cleaning and safety.

Nuts and Bolts

Table mixers

Make sure that the speed switch on the machine is set at zero or off before plugging in and turning on the mains switch to start mixing.

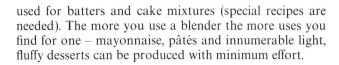

Beater, whisk and dough hook for a table mixer

Check that the bowl and beaters are firmly fixed in position.

Check in the manufacturer's instruction booklet for the maximum and minimum quantities for satisfactory results.

Switch on at the mains, place the ingredients in the bowl and then turn the switch to the correct speed for the recipe.

Scrape the mixture from the sides of the bowl during mixing, if necessary, with a rubber or plastic spatula.

Be careful not to over mix.

Make sure any attachment used is correctly fitted.

Food processors

Check that the bowl is firmly in position on the base before using the machine.

Turn on at the mains switch before using the switch on the machine (this is often operated by a locking device on the lid).

Know the capacity of your machine and never overload it.

Be careful not to over process; most processing is done in seconds rather than minutes.

For even chopping, process by operating the switch in short bursts rather than letting it run continuously. Some machines have a 'burst' switch button.

When tipping processed food out of the bowl, it is easier to get a grip and keeps the blade in position if you put your thumb up the hole. Some bowls have a handle.

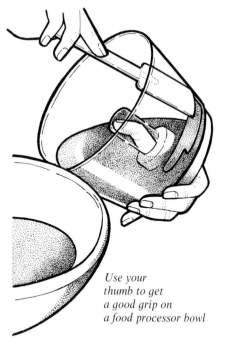

Use your thumb to get a good grip on a food processor bowl

Hand mixers

Make sure the switch or speed dial on the machine is at zero or off before plugging in and switching on at the mains.

If using a hand mixer with its own stand and bowl, check the capacity of the machine before adding the ingredients.

When using a mixer on a stand, stop the motor occasionally during mixing and scrape the mixture from the sides of the bowl with a rubber or plastic spatula.

When using the mixer hand held, move it gently round the bowl as the beaters rotate.

Remember that it is possible to use a hand held mixer in any suitably sized bowl, jug or saucepan.

Turn the switch on the mixer off before removing the beaters from the mixture.

Blenders

Check that the goblet and lid are firmly in position before switching the blender on.

A hand mixer can be used over the cooker

17

Turn on the mains switch before using the switch on the machine.

Check on the capacity of the goblet and never overload it. For liquids, the capacity is three-quarters of the brimful capacity, and this is usually marked on the goblet. For thick mixtures, half full is the normal recommendation.

Run the motor only for one minute at a time. After a minute of blending, switch off the machine and wait for a few seconds before completing the process. Some machines have a 'burst' switch button.

If the contents are not mixing properly, try turning off the machine and shaking the contents gently, or remove some of the mixture, or shift the food around in the goblet with a rubber spatula.

Process food thoroughly before adding any more.

If the processed food cannot be poured out of the goblet, use a rubber or plastic spatula.

Different Mixtures, Different Measures

Table mixers

For creamed cake mixtures and cream fillings, use ingredients at room temperature and warm the bowl and beaters in hot water. Fold flour into creamed mixtures at a low speed and be careful to switch off as soon as the flour is incorporated. Overdoing the mixing at this stage results in a heavy cake.

When rubbing fat into flour for pastry and plain cakes, have all the ingredients, bowl and beaters as cold as possible. Fat can be taken straight from the refrigerator. Once again, be careful not to over mix; rubbing in normally takes seconds only.

To whisk egg whites, be sure the bowl and beaters are absolutely clean.

To whip cream, start on maximum speed but reduce the speed as soon as the cream starts to thicken to avoid overbeating and turning the cream to butter.

Leave royal icing to stand overnight in a refrigerator, well covered with polythene. This allows any air bubbles trapped in the mixture to escape and results in a smoother icing.

Warm the dough hook and bowl in hot water before adding raw ingredients.

Cut food to the size recommended in the instructions before placing it in the shredder, slicer, mincer or juice separator. To get the maximum juice from the juice separator, take the trouble to remove the pulp and rinse the filters between processing separate batches of fruit or vegetables.

Food processors

When chopping raw meat, remember that over processing produces meat paste rather than mince; eight seconds is the average time required to mince 450 g (1 lb) raw meat.

Cut fats into 2.5-cm (1-in) pieces for cake making and have all the ingredients at room temperature.

Use fat straight from the refrigerator for pastry making and be certain not to over process. Pastry is best if chilled for 30 minutes in the refrigerator after mixing and before rolling out.

Always add liquids to a mixture through a feed tube.

It is usually necessary to allow boiling liquids to cool slightly before pouring them into the bowl.

When using a juice extractor attachment be sure to clear the residue from the bowl before fresh pieces of fruit or vegetable are added.

When making a one-egg mayonnaise it may be necessary to tip the machine slightly on one end so that the blades cut through the mixture and a good result is achieved.

Ice cubes may be crushed in liquid in most food processors (check instructions for individual machines) but doing it frequently blunts the knife blades.

Grinding coffee beans is not usually recommended (again, check instructions for individual machines) both because it blunts the blades and leaves a lingering smell. In an emergency it is usually possible to grind a small amount.

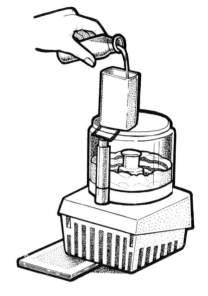

Tilt your food processor when making only a small amount of mayonnaise

Hand mixers

When creaming ingredients for a cake or cream filling, have the ingredients at room temperature and warm the bowl – either the one that goes with the machine or an independent bowl.

For pastry, keep the bowl and ingredients cool.

A bowl with straightish sides is usually best for cake mixtures.

Small quantities of mixture are often mixed more satisfactorily in a small straight-sided bowl than by using the bowl and stand provided with the mixer.

Blenders

For blending liquids or semi-liquids, fill the goblet according to recommended capacity, fix the lid and switch to low speed, increasing to high. With some heavy mixtures it is recommended to switch directly to a high speed.

19

Allow steam to escape from a blender by tipping the stopper

If thick mixtures are not combining well, add a little more liquid.

To process solids, for example cheese or breadcrumbs, switch the motor on, remove the lid stopper and drop 1-cm ($\frac{1}{2}$-in) pieces of the ingredient on to the revolving blade, a few at a time. A high speed is normally recommended. Process the pieces thoroughly before adding any more.

For hot ingredients, start at a low speed and vent the lid by tipping *the stopper only* slightly to one side. Never remove the lid itself while the machine is working.

Check instructions before grinding coffee in your blender. It is only recommended in an emergency as it blunts the blades. Both coffee and spices leave a lingering smell.

Ice may be crushed in liquid in some machines to make drinks (check instructions) but ice cubes alone should not be crushed in the goblet – a special ice crusher is usually necessary.

Keep it Clean

Never put the machine part of your mixer into water. Wipe it over with a damp cloth and polish it dry.

Wash bowls, blender goblets, beaters, blades and attachments in hot soapy water and then rinse. Blender goblets are easier to wash if they are first filled three-quarters full of warm water and switched on for a few seconds. For blenders with removable blades, take the goblet and blades apart for washing, taking special care not to cut your fingers. Avoid using abrasives to clean your mixer.

Dry everything thoroughly, especially metal blades and attachments. Again, take care with sharp blades. Never dry plastic bowls, goblets, blades or attachments in the oven or on top of the cooker.

Don't wash plastic bowls, goblets, blades or attachments in a dishwasher unless directed otherwise.

Remove the pusher of a food processor or vent the lid of a plastic blender goblet before storing. This allows air to circulate and prevents a smell developing.

Protect your machine from dust when not in use.

Safety Rules

Whatever type of appliance you have, don't use it too near the edge of the work surface or table. Avoid having too long an electric lead on the machine as trailing flexes can cause accidents. Be sure that the electric plug is correctly wired and fitted with the fuse recommended in the instruction leaflet. Unplug the machine after use and before cleaning.

Table mixers
Turn the speed control switch to off or zero after use as well as turning off the mains switch.
Never put an implement or your fingers into the bowl while the beaters are rotating.
Never push food on to the slicing, shredding or mincing attachments with your fingers.

Food processors
Never leave the bowl in the switched on position after you have used the machine. This applies particularly to the type with the lid-lock switch.
Always press food through the feed tube on to the grating or slicing disc with the pusher. Never be tempted to use your fingers.
Never put your fingers through the feed tube while the blades are in position.
Always wait until the blades have stopped turning before taking the lid off the bowl.
Handle the blades with care, always holding them with the knob or holder provided, and store them well out of the reach of children.
Don't pour boiling liquids into the bowl unless otherwise directed.

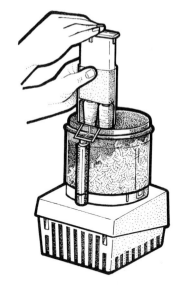
Use the feed tube, never your fingers

Hand mixers
When using the mixer hand held in a saucepan or basin over a pan of water on the cooker, check that the flex does not trail across the hot plate or burner.
When using a mixer on a stand, always keep an eye on it as it is working as it will not be quite as stable as a traditional table mixer.

Blenders
Make sure that the motor is switched off at the wall switch and on the machine itself before attaching the goblet.
Never use the blender without the lid in position.
Never take the lid off before the blades have stopped turning.
Never put your fingers into the goblet while the motor is switched on.
Removable blade bases should be handled with great care and kept out of the reach of children.
To protect the blades, don't put the removable blade base on to the motor without putting the goblet on it as well.
Don't pour boiling liquids into the goblet unless otherwise directed.
Never leave a blender working unattended.

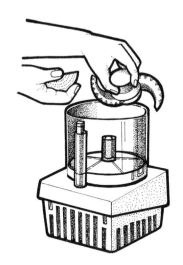
Handle the blades of a food processor with care

21

Soups
and
Starters

Summer soup

10 small spring onions, trimmed
600 ml (1 pint) chicken stock
1 medium lettuce, washed
1 bunch watercress, washed
salt and freshly ground pepper
150 ml ($\frac{1}{4}$ pint) natural yogurt
15 ml (1 tbsp) lemon juice
croûtons to garnish

Chop the onions and place in a large saucepan with the stock. Bring to the boil and simmer gently for 10 minutes. Shred the lettuce and chop the watercress and add to the pan with the seasoning. Cover and continue to cook for 10 minutes. Blend the soup to form a purée. Leave to cool and chill thoroughly.

Beat the yogurt and lemon juice into the chilled soup, then pour into a tureen and serve garnished with the croûtons.
Serves 4

To freeze Cool the purée and pour into a rigid container. To serve, thaw overnight in the refrigerator, or at room temperature for 5 hours, then add the yogurt, lemon juice and croûtons as above.

Onion egg soup

75 g (3 oz) butter
700 g (1$\frac{1}{2}$ lb) onions, skinned
1 garlic clove, skinned and crushed
40 g (1$\frac{1}{2}$ oz) flour
1.1 litre (2 pints) beef stock
bay leaf
salt and freshly ground pepper
75 g (3 oz) Cheddar cheese
2 eggs, beaten
6 slices French bread, toasted

Melt the butter in a saucepan. Thinly slice the onion and add to the pan with the garlic. Fry gently for 10 minutes until golden brown. Stir in the flour and cook for 1–2 minutes until lightly browned. Gradually stir in the stock then bring the soup to the boil, stirring all the time. Add the bay leaf and seasoning, cover and simmer gently for 30 minutes.

Remove the bay leaf. Finely grate the cheese and mix with the egg. Remove the soup from the heat and beat in the egg mixture. Place the toast in a warm tureen and pour over the soup.
Serves 6

To freeze Cool and pour into a rigid container, omitting the egg and cheese mixture and the toast. To serve, put the frozen soup in a saucepan and reheat gently. Add the egg and cheese mixture and toast as above.

Broccoli orange soup

25 g (1 oz) butter
1 medium onion, skinned
600 ml (1 pint) chicken stock
900 g (2 lb) broccoli, trimmed
juice of 1 orange
salt and freshly ground pepper
60 ml (4 tbsp) double cream
2 thin orange slices, halved, to garnish

Melt the butter in a large saucepan, slice the onion and fry gently for 5 minutes until soft. Add the stock, broccoli, orange juice and seasoning. Cover and simmer for 20 minutes until the broccoli is tender. Blend the soup to form a purée. Return to the pan and heat through. Remove from the heat and stir in the cream. Garnish each bowl with a slice of orange.
Serves 4

To freeze Cool and pour into a rigid container, omitting the cream and garnish. To serve, put the frozen soup in a saucepan and reheat gently, stirring in the cream and garnishing as above.

Vegetable beef soup

1 medium onion, skinned
100 g (4 oz) carrot, peeled
100 g (4 oz) potato, peeled
50 g (2 oz) turnip, peeled
50 g (2 oz) swede, peeled
50 g (2 oz) leek, trimmed
226-g (8-oz) can tomatoes
15 ml (1 level tbsp) tomato purée
5 ml (1 tsp) Worcestershire sauce
600 ml (1 pint) beef stock
salt and freshly ground pepper
175 g (6 oz) lean beef
chopped fresh parsley to garnish

Coarsely chop the onion and carrot, dice the potato, turnip and swede and slice and wash the leek. Place all the vegetables in a large saucepan with the tomato purée, Worcestershire sauce, stock and seasoning. Bring to the boil, cover and simmer gently for 45 minutes. Blend the vegetables to form a purée and return to the pan.

Mince the beef, add to the soup and cook for 20 minutes. Pour into a warm serving bowl and garnish with the parsley.
Serves 4

To freeze Cool and pour into a rigid container, omitting the garnish. To serve, put the

frozen soup in a saucepan and reheat gently. Garnish as above.

Salami coleslaw

225 g (8 oz) white cabbage
$\frac{1}{2}$ red pepper, seeded
1 small onion, skinned
175 g (6 oz) salami
30 ml (2 tbsp) chopped fresh parsley
150 ml ($\frac{1}{4}$ pint) soured cream
15 ml (1 tbsp) wine vinegar
salt and freshly ground pepper
10 ml (2 level tsp) Dijon mustard
1 bunch watercress, washed

Slice the cabbage and chop the pepper and onion finely. Dice the salami. Mix together with the parsley in a large bowl. Blend the soured cream, vinegar, seasoning and mustard together until smooth. Pour the dressing over the salad and mix well. Arrange the watercress on a serving plate and spoon the salad over. Chill before serving.
Serves 4

Not suitable for freezing

A blender is particularly useful for soups

25

Cheese and bacon ramekins

15 g ($\frac{1}{2}$ oz) butter
100 g (4 oz) back bacon rashers, rinded
50 g (2 oz) button mushrooms, wiped
225 g (8 oz) cottage cheese
60 ml (4 tbsp) milk
2.5 ml ($\frac{1}{2}$ level tsp) ground coriander
salt and freshly ground pepper
sliced tomato to garnish

Melt the butter in a frying pan and fry the bacon rashers for 10 minutes until crisp and golden brown. Add the mushrooms and cook for 5 minutes.

Blend the bacon and mushrooms and all the remaining ingredients together to form a purée. Spoon into four individual dishes and chill for 1 hour. Garnish with tomato slices and serve with fingers of toast.
Serves 4

To freeze Pack in a rigid container, omitting the garnish; alternatively cover the individual dishes. To serve, thaw overnight in a refrigerator, or at·room temperature for 3 hours and garnish as above.

Pasta and chicken soup

1 medium onion, skinned
25 g (1 oz) butter
1 large potato, peeled
1 large carrot, peeled
900 ml (1$\frac{1}{2}$ pints) chicken stock
salt and freshly ground pepper
225 g (8 oz) cooked chicken
50 g (2 oz) small shell-shaped pasta
100 g (4 oz) frozen sweetcorn
100 g (4 oz) frozen peas
5 ml (1 level tsp) dried marjoram
chopped fresh parsley to garnish

Finely slice the onion and fry gently in the butter in a large saucepan for 10 minutes until soft. Chop the potato and carrot and cook with the onion for a further 5 minutes. Add the

chicken stock and seasoning, then bring to the boil, cover and simmer for 20 minutes.

Chop the chicken; add to the soup with the pasta, sweetcorn, peas and marjoram. Cover and cook for a further 10 minutes. Pour into a warm serving bowl and garnish with parsley.
Serves 6

To freeze Cool and pour into a rigid container. To serve, thaw for 3–4 hours at room temperature. Reheat gently in a saucepan, adding 300 ml ($\frac{1}{2}$ pint) extra chicken stock, and garnish as above.

Avocado Creams

Illustrated in colour facing page 32

$\frac{1}{2}$ small onion, skinned
2 medium avocados, halved, stoned and skinned
grated rind of $\frac{1}{2}$ a lemon
45 ml (3 tbsp) lemon juice
150 ml ($\frac{1}{4}$ pint) mayonnaise (see page 63)
salt and freshly ground pepper
150 ml ($\frac{1}{4}$ pint) double cream
sprigs of watercress to garnish

Finely chop the onion. Blend the avocado flesh, lemon rind and juice, mayonnaise, seasoning and onion together to form a purée. Whisk the cream until thick. Fold the avocado mixture into the cream. Spoon the avocado cream into six small soufflé dishes, chill for 1

26

hour and serve garnished with sprigs of watercress. Eat the same day, with fingers of toast. *Serves 6*

Not suitable for freezing

Taramasalata

1 small onion, skinned
225 g (8 oz) smoked cod's roe
1 garlic clove, skinned and crushed
50 g (2 oz) fresh white breadcrumbs
grated rind and juice of 1 lemon
150 ml ($\frac{1}{4}$ pint) olive oil
freshly ground pepper
30 ml (2 tbsp) chopped fresh parsley
lemon slices to garnish

Finely chop the onion. Skin the cod's roe and break into pieces. Blend to form a purée. Add the garlic, breadcrumbs, onion and lemon rind and juice and blend for a few more seconds. Gradually add the oil and blend well after each addition until smooth. Blend in 90 ml (6 tbsp) hot water with the pepper and parsley. Spoon into a serving dish and chill for at least 1 hour. Garnish with lemon slices and serve with toast. *Serves 6*

Not suitable for freezing

Lettuce and ham soup

15 g ($\frac{1}{2}$ oz) butter
1 medium onion, skinned
1 large lettuce, washed
600 ml (1 pint) ham or chicken stock
salt and freshly ground pepper
5 ml (1 level tsp) sugar
100 g (4 oz) cooked gammon steak
croûtons to garnish

Melt the butter in a large saucepan, chop the onion and cook for 5 minutes until soft. Shred the lettuce, add to the onion with the stock and simmer for 10 minutes. Blend for a few seconds

to form a purée and return to the pan. Stir in the seasoning and sugar. Dice the gammon and add to the soup, then cover and simmer gently for 15 minutes. Pour into a warm soup tureen and garnish with the croûtons. *Serves 4*

To freeze Cool and pour into a rigid container, omitting the garnish. To serve, put the frozen soup in a saucepan and reheat gently. Garnish as above.

Salad ham ring

2 Webb lettuces, washed
25 g (1 oz) powdered gelatine
225 g (8 oz) cooked ham
1 medium onion, skinned
150 ml ($\frac{1}{4}$ pint) mayonnaise (see page 63)
1 egg, separated
150 ml ($\frac{1}{4}$ pint) soured cream
salt and freshly ground pepper
10 ml (2 tsp) Worcestershire sauce
watercress to garnish

Shred the lettuces and cook for 10 minutes in a large saucepan in the water remaining on the leaves. Purée the lettuce and leave to cool. In a small bowl, sprinkle the gelatine over 45 ml (3 tbsp) water. Stand the bowl over a saucepan of hot water and heat gently until dissolved. Cool, then stir into the lettuce purée.

Mince the ham and onion and mix with the mayonnaise, egg yolk, soured cream, seasoning and Worcestershire sauce. Stir the mixture into the lettuce purée. Whisk the egg white until stiff and fold into the lettuce mixture. Pour into a lightly oiled 1.4-litre ($2\frac{1}{2}$-pint) ring mould and place in the refrigerator to set. Unmould and garnish with watercress. *Serves 6*

To freeze Wrap the mousse before unmoulding. To serve, thaw at room temperature for 4 hours. Unmould and garnish as above.

Horseradish mackerel pâté

**350 g (12 oz) smoked mackerel, skinned and
boned**
105 ml (7 level tbsp) soured cream
45 ml (3 level tbsp) creamed horseradish
salt and freshly ground pepper
75 g (3 oz) cottage cheese
10 ml (2 tsp) chopped fresh chives
15 ml (1 tbsp) lemon juice
tomato slices to garnish

Blend all the ingredients together to form a
purée. Spoon into four individual dishes and
chill for 1 hour. Garnish with tomato slices and
serve with warm toast or crusty French bread.
Serves 4

To freeze Omit the garnish and pack the pâté
into a rigid container or cover the individual
dishes. To serve, thaw overnight in a refrigerator or at room temperature for 5 hours and
garnish as above.

Iced tomato soup

450 g (1 lb) ripe tomatoes
1 medium onion, skinned
20 ml (4 level tsp) tomato purée
411-g (14½-oz) can chicken consommé
5 ml (1 level tsp) dried basil
15 g (½ oz) fresh white breadcrumbs
150 ml (¼ pint) soured cream
spring onion tops or chives to garnish

Chop the tomatoes and onion and blend together with the tomato purée, consommé and
basil to form a purée. Pour into a bowl and stir
in the breadcrumbs. Cover and chill well before
serving. Spoon into individual dishes, add
swirls of soured cream and garnish with a few
snipped spring onion tops or chives.
Serves 4

To freeze Pour into a rigid container, omitting
the cream and garnish. To serve, thaw in a
refrigerator for 4 hours and garnish as above.

Courgette and mushroom soup

700 g (1½ lb) courgettes, trimmed
1.1 litre (2 pints) chicken stock
salt and freshly ground pepper
175 g (6 oz) mushrooms
15 ml (1 tbsp) chopped fresh parsley
25 g (1 oz) Parmesan cheese
croûtons to garnish

Slice the courgettes and place in a large
saucepan with the stock and seasoning. Cover
and simmer for 25 minutes until tender. Slice
the mushrooms, add to the soup and continue
cooking for 10 minutes. Blend the vegetables to
form a purée. Return to the saucepan to heat
through and add the parsley. Grate the cheese.
Pour the soup into a warm serving bowl,
sprinkle over the cheese and garnish with the
croûtons.
Serves 4

To freeze Cool and pour into a rigid container, omitting the garnish. To serve, put the
frozen soup in a saucepan and reheat gently,
garnishing as above.

Sorrel soup

25 g (1 oz) butter
1 medium onion, skinned
100 g (4 oz) fresh sorrel leaves, washed
225 g (8 oz) potatoes, peeled
900 ml (1½ pints) chicken stock
salt and freshly ground pepper
150 ml (¼ pint) soured cream

Melt the butter in a saucepan, chop the onion
and fry for 5 minutes until soft. Shred the sorrel
leaves and cook with the onion for a further
2–3 minutes. Chop the potatoes and add
with the stock and seasoning, then cover and
simmer gently for 20 minutes. Blend to form a
purée, then return to the pan and reheat. Pour
into a warm serving bowl and swirl the cream
on top.
Serves 4

To freeze Cool and pour into a rigid container, omitting the soured cream. To serve,

place the frozen soup in a saucepan, reheat gently and add the soured cream as above.

Fisherman's pâté

700 g (1½ lb) smoked haddock fillets
150 ml (¼ pint) milk
salt and freshly ground pepper
grated rind and juice of ½ a lemon
pinch of ground mace
60 ml (4 tbsp) double cream
4 whole prawns to garnish

Place the haddock in a saucepan with the milk and poach for 15 minutes until the fish flakes easily. Remove the fish from the pan, reserving the liquid. Remove the skin and any bones and blend with 90 ml (6 tbsp) of the cooking liquid to form a purée. Stir in the seasoning, lemon rind and juice, mace and double cream. Spoon into a serving dish and chill for 1 hour. Garnish with the prawns and serve with fingers of toast.
Serves 4

To freeze Pack in a rigid container, omitting the garnish. To serve, thaw overnight in a refrigerator, or at room temperature for 5 hours, and garnish as above.

Caraway cabbage soup

450 g (1 lb) spring cabbage
1 large onion, skinned
900 ml (1½ pints) chicken stock
300 ml (½ pint) tomato juice
30 ml (2 level tbsp) tomato purée
salt and freshly ground pepper
2.5 ml (½ level tsp) caraway seeds
30 ml (2 level tbsp) cornflour
60 ml (4 level tbsp) soured cream

Shred the cabbage and chop the onion finely. Place the cabbage, onion, stock, tomato juice, tomato purée, seasoning and caraway seeds in

a large saucepan. Cover, bring to the boil and simmer gently for 20 minutes until the cabbage is tender. Blend the cornflour with a little water to form a paste and add to the soup. Bring to the boil again, stirring until thickened and cook for a few minutes. Remove from the heat and pour into a warm serving bowl. Leave to stand for 5 minutes, then spoon the soured cream on to the soup and serve.
Serves 6

To freeze Cool and pour into a rigid container, omitting the soured cream. To serve, put the frozen soup into a saucepan, reheat gently and stir in the soured cream as above.

Egg and anchovy mousse

For the first course of a summer meal this egg mousse is lighter than a meat pâté. Serve with freshly made brown toast fingers tucked into a napkin.

90 ml (6 level tbsp) mayonnaise (see page 63)
1 egg, separated
8 anchovy fillets
freshly ground pepper
30 ml (2 tbsp) single cream
5 ml (1 tsp) anchovy essence
few drops Tabasco sauce
4 hard-boiled eggs
1 tomato, sliced, and watercress to garnish

Blend together the mayonnaise, egg yolk, anchovy fillets, seasoning, cream, anchovy essence and Tabasco to form a purée. Shell the hard-boiled eggs, chop finely and add to the anchovy mixture. Whisk the egg white until stiff and carefully fold into the mousse. Spoon the mousse into a serving dish and chill in the refrigerator for 2 hours until firm. Garnish with the tomato slices and watercress.
Serves 4

Not suitable for freezing

Tomato bacon soup

100 g (4 oz) smoked bacon rashers, rinded
1 large onion, skinned
4 sticks of celery, washed
30 ml (2 level tbsp) tomato purée
1.1 litre (2 pints) ham stock
226-g (8-oz) can tomatoes
175 g (6 oz) split yellow lentils, washed
1 bay leaf
salt and freshly ground pepper
450 g (1 lb) potatoes, peeled
lemon juice to taste
chopped fresh parsley to garnish

Chop the bacon and fry in a large saucepan in its own fat for 5 minutes. Chop the onion and celery, add to the pan with the tomato purée and cook for 10 minutes. Pour in the stock with the tomatoes, lentils, bay leaf and seasoning. Bring to the boil, then cover and simmer for about 1 hour until the lentils are soft.

Dice the potatoes, add to the soup and cook for a further 20 minutes. Remove the bay leaf from the soup and blend to form a purée. Add lemon juice to taste and reheat gently. Serve sprinkled with parsley.
Serves 4

To freeze Cool and pour into a rigid container, omitting the garnish. To serve, put the frozen soup in a saucepan, reheat gently and garnish as above.

Tuna herb bisque

1 medium onion, skinned
1 small green pepper, seeded
2 sticks of celery, washed
1 large potato, peeled
300 ml ($\frac{1}{2}$ pint) milk
600 ml (1 pint) fish or chicken stock
salt and freshly ground pepper
30 ml (2 tbsp) chopped fresh herbs
30 ml (2 tbsp) lemon juice
198-g (7-oz) can tuna, drained and flaked
15 ml (1 level tbsp) cornflour
chopped fresh chives to garnish

Chop the onion, green pepper and celery and dice the potato. Place all the vegetables in a large saucepan with the milk, stock and seasoning. Bring to the boil, cover and simmer gently for 40 minutes. Blend the vegetables to form a purée and return to the pan.

Add the herbs, lemon juice and tuna. Blend the cornflour with a little water to form a paste and add to the soup. Bring to the boil, stirring until thickened slightly, and cook for 2 minutes. Pour into a warm serving bowl and sprinkle with chives to garnish.
Serves 4

To freeze Make the vegetable purée, cool and pour into a rigid container. To serve, put the frozen soup into a large saucepan and heat gently until thawed, then follow the rest of the recipe.

Shrimp puffs

$\frac{1}{2}$ small onion, skinned
15 g ($\frac{1}{2}$ oz) butter
15 ml (1 level tbsp) flour
50 ml (2 fl oz) milk
1 egg, beaten
10 ml (2 tsp) chopped fresh parsley
15 ml (1 level tbsp) finely chopped gherkin
75 g (3 oz) peeled shrimps
15 ml (1 tbsp) lemon juice
5 ml (1 level tsp) grated lemon rind
salt and freshly ground pepper
dash of Tabasco sauce
175 g (6 oz) frozen puff pastry, thawed
milk to glaze
lemon wedges and parsley to garnish

Finely chop the onion. Blend the butter, flour and milk together until smooth and pour into a saucepan with the onion. Cook gently for 2 minutes, stirring continuously until the sauce thickens. Remove from the heat and stir in the egg, parsley, gherkin, shrimps, lemon juice and rind, seasoning and Tabasco sauce.

Roll out the pastry and cut into six 7.5-cm (3-in) squares. Divide the filling equally between

Grate the cucumber. Add the mint, garlic, yogurt and seasoning. Cover and chill. Just before serving stir in the milk. Serve in a tureen, garnished with mint leaves.
Serves 4

To freeze Pour into a rigid container, omitting the garnish. To serve, thaw in the refrigerator for 4 hours, garnishing as above.

Chilled mushroom and lemon soup

This smooth, sharp-tasting purée of mushrooms has the consistency of cream and should be served really cold. If the weather is very warm, chill the soup bowls in the refrigerator and add an ice cube to each serving.

450 g (1 lb) flat mushrooms, wiped
grated rind of 1 lemon
45 ml (3 tbsp) lemon juice
1 garlic clove, skinned and crushed
salt and freshly ground pepper
10 ml (2 tsp) chopped fresh thyme
900 ml (1½ pints) chicken stock
150 ml (¼ pint) single cream
chopped fresh parsley to garnish

Slice two mushrooms and reserve for the garnish. Chop the remaining mushrooms and place in a flat dish with the lemon rind and juice, garlic, seasoning and thyme. Leave to marinate for 2 hours, turning the mushrooms occasionally. Blend the mushrooms, marinade and stock to form a purée and stir in the cream. Adjust the seasoning and chill well before serving. Garnish with the reserved mushroom slices and chopped parsley.
Serves 6–8

To freeze Pour into a rigid container, omitting the cream and parsley. To serve, thaw in the refrigerator for 4 hours, stir in the chilled cream and garnish.

the pastry squares, dampen the edges with water and fold in half to form a triangle. Seal the edges and place on a greased baking tray. Glaze with the milk. Bake in the oven at 200°C (400°F) mark 6 for 30 minutes until well risen and golden brown. Serve hot, garnished with lemon wedges and parsley.
Serves 6

To freeze Cool and pack in a rigid container. To serve, place on a greased baking tray while frozen and reheat in the oven at 190°C (375°F) mark 5 for about 30 minutes until warmed through.

Iced cucumber mint soup

Illustrated in colour on the jacket

A light refreshing soup for hot summer days.

1 large cucumber, washed but not peeled
30 ml (2 tbsp) chopped fresh mint
1 garlic clove, skinned and chopped
300 ml (½ pint) natural yogurt
salt and white pepper
300 ml (½ pint) ice cold milk
mint leaves to garnish

Aubergine parsley starter

Illustrated in colour opposite

700 g (1½ lb) aubergines
25 g (1 oz) butter
1 large onion, skinned
1 garlic clove, skinned and crushed
15 g (½ oz) fresh parsley
30 ml (2 tbsp) lemon juice
salt and freshly ground pepper
150 ml (¼ pint) vegetable oil
chopped parsley to garnish

Prick the skins of the aubergines and place on a greased baking tray. Bake in the oven at 190°C (375°F) mark 5 for 45 minutes until soft. Cool slightly, cut in half and scoop out the flesh. Meanwhile melt the butter in a pan, chop the onion and fry the onion and garlic for 10 minutes until soft. Add the aubergine flesh and fry for a further 5 minutes.

Blend the fried aubergine mixture, parsley, lemon juice and seasoning to form a purée. Gradually add the oil, beating well after each addition. Chill for 1 hour. Serve the aubergine starter with fingers of toast, garnished with chopped parsley.
Serves 6

To freeze Pack in a rigid container. To serve, thaw in the refrigerator overnight, or at room temperature for 4 hours. Prepare the toast and garnish as above.

Cream of celery soup with peanuts

1 large head of celery, washed and trimmed
1 medium onion, skinned
100 g (4 oz) margarine
1.4 litres (2½ pints) chicken stock
salt and freshly ground pepper
2.5 ml (½ level tsp) dried basil
75 g (3 oz) salted peanuts
150 ml (¼ pint) milk
60 ml (4 level tbsp) flour

Slice the celery and onion. Melt half the margarine in a saucepan, add the celery and onion, cover and cook gently for about 20 minutes until tender. Add the stock, seasoning and basil, bring to the boil and simmer for 30 minutes. Blend to form a purée.

Chop the peanuts. Bring the milk to the boil and add the peanuts, then remove from the heat and leave to infuse until required. Blend the remaining margarine, the flour and puréed celery mixture together until smooth. Pour into a saucepan, stir in the milk and nuts and heat through. Adjust the seasoning and serve.
Serves 4

To freeze Cool and pour into a rigid container, omitting the milk and nuts. To serve, reheat the frozen soup gently in a saucepan and add the milk and nuts as above.

Smoked salmon mousse

1 small carrot, washed
1 small onion, skinned
300 ml (½ pint) milk
3 parsley stalks
6 peppercorns
40 g (1½ oz) butter
25 g (1 oz) flour
100 g (4 oz) smoked salmon trimmings
25 ml (5 level tsp) powdered gelatine
400 ml (¾ pint) chicken stock
juice of ½ a lemon
30 ml (2 level tbsp) mayonnaise
    (see page 63)
150 ml (¼ pint) double cream
salt and freshly ground pepper
lemon slices and small rolls of smoked
    salmon to garnish

Chop the carrot and halve the onion. Pour the milk into a saucepan and add the carrot, onion, parsley stalks and peppercorns. Bring to the boil, then remove from the heat and allow to infuse for 15 minutes. Strain and reserve the milk.
Blend the butter, flour and strained milk to-

32

Hummus (page 62), Aubergine parsley starter (above),
Avocado creams (page 26)

gether until smooth. Pour into a saucepan, bring to the boil and cook gently, stirring, for 2–3 minutes until thickened. Cover the sauce with greaseproof paper and leave to cool.

Chop the smoked salmon. In a small bowl, sprinkle the gelatine over 45 ml (3 tbsp) of the stock and stand it over a pan of hot water, heating gently until dissolved. Add the rest of the stock and leave to cool. Fold the gelatine mixture into the white sauce. Add the smoked salmon, lemon juice and mayonnaise. Whip the cream lightly and fold it into the salmon mixture. Season to taste. Pour the mixture into a 15-cm (6-in) soufflé dish or a 1.1-litre (2-pint) mould. Leave to set. To turn out, dip the container in hot water and invert on to a serving plate. Garnish with lemon slices and small rolls of smoked salmon. Serve with Melba toast.
Serves 6

To freeze Cover the mousse before turning out. To serve, thaw at room temperature for about 4 hours. Unmould and garnish as above.

English pea soup

450 g (1 lb) shelled peas
900 ml (1½ pints) chicken stock
2 parsley sprigs
2 mint sprigs
2.5 ml (½ level tsp) granulated sugar
3 spring onions, trimmed
50 g (2 oz) butter
15 g (½ oz) flour
300 ml (½ pint) milk
salt and freshly ground pepper
chopped fresh mint or spring onion
**   tops to garnish**

Put the peas, stock, parsley, mint, sugar and onions in a large saucepan. Cover and simmer for about 40 minutes until the peas are soft. Remove the parsley, mint and spring onions and blend the peas and stock to form a purée. Blend the butter, flour and milk together until smooth. Pour into a saucepan and bring to the boil, stirring all the time, to thicken. Cook

gently for 2–3 minutes. Stir in the pea purée and reheat gently. Add seasoning to taste. Serve garnished with chopped mint or spring onion tops.
Serves 6

To freeze Cool and pour into a rigid container, omitting the garnish. To serve, reheat the frozen soup gently in a saucepan and garnish as above.

Flan provençal (page 57)

Main Meals

Sausage and bacon savoury en croûte

Illustrated in colour on the jacket

1 large onion, skinned
25 g (1 oz) butter
450 g (1 lb) streaky bacon rashers, rinded
175 g (6 oz) fresh white breadcrumbs
50 g (2 oz) shredded suet
15 ml (1 tbsp) chopped fresh parsley
salt and freshly ground pepper
1 egg, beaten
175 g (6 oz) cooked chicken
350 g (12 oz) sausagemeat
369-g (13-oz) packet frozen puff pastry, thawed
beaten egg to glaze

Chop the onion. Melt the butter in a saucepan and fry the onion for about 5 minutes until soft. Reserve eight rashers of bacon and chop the rest. Add the chopped bacon to the onion and continue to cook for 5 minutes. Mix the onion and bacon with the breadcrumbs, suet, parsley and seasoning. Bind together with the egg.

Stretch the reserved bacon rashers with the back of a knife on a wooden board, and use six to line the base and sides of a 900-g (2-lb) loaf tin or pâté dish. Reserve two rashers for the top. Slice the chicken. Spread half the sausagemeat over the base and cover with half the chicken. Add the bacon and onion mixture, then the remaining chicken, and finish with a layer of sausagemeat. Top with the reserved bacon rashers. Cover with foil and stand the tin in a roasting tin half filled with hot water. Bake in the oven at 180°C (350°F) mark 4 for 1½ hours. Remove from the roasting tin and leave until cold.

Roll out the pastry thinly on a lightly floured surface. Brush with beaten egg. Remove the sausage and bacon loaf from the tin and wrap in the pastry. Seal the edges well and brush with egg. Use any pastry trimmings to decorate the top. Place on a baking tray and cook in the oven at 200°C (400°F) mark 6 for 35 minutes until golden brown and well risen. Leave until cold before serving.
Serves 8

To freeze Wrap and freeze before covering with pastry. Allow to thaw in a refrigerator overnight then wrap in pastry and bake as above.

Beef and tomato herb cobbler

1 large onion, skinned
75 g (3 oz) butter
450 g (1 lb) lean beef
100 g (4 oz) button mushrooms, wiped
25 g (1 oz) plain flour
150 ml (¼ pint) red wine
30 ml (2 level tbsp) tomato purée
396-g (14-oz) can tomatoes
salt and freshly ground pepper
225 g (8 oz) self raising flour
30 ml (2 tbsp) chopped fresh herbs
150 ml (¼ pint) milk
beaten egg to glaze

Chop the onion. Melt 25 g (1 oz) butter in a large saucepan and fry the onion gently for 10 minutes until soft. Mince the beef and slice the mushrooms. Add to the onion and cook for 10 minutes, stirring. Add the flour and cook for 2 minutes then gradually add the wine, stirring to thicken. Stir in the tomato purée, canned

tomatoes and seasoning. Cover and simmer gently for 20 minutes.

Meanwhile make the topping. Add a pinch of salt to the flour and mix in the remaining butter, until it resembles fine breadcrumbs. Add the herbs and milk and mix to a soft dough. Roll out to 1 cm ($\frac{1}{2}$ in) thick and using a 4-cm ($1\frac{1}{2}$-in) cutter cut into eight rounds. Pour the beef mixture into an ovenproof dish and top with the scone rounds. Brush the scones with beaten egg and bake in the oven at 200°C (400°F) mark 6 for 25 minutes until the cobbler topping has risen and is golden brown. *Serves 4*

To freeze Cool meat mixture quickly then pack in a rigid container. Wrap the scone mixture in foil. To serve, thaw meat and scone topping in the refrigerator overnight, then continue as above.

Tarragon fish pie

**350 g (12 oz) shortcrust pastry
(see page 57 and double the quantity)
1 small onion, skinned
50 g (2 oz) butter
50 g (2 oz) flour
568 ml (1 pint) milk
salt and freshly ground pepper
450 g (1 lb) cod fillet
4 hard-boiled eggs
15 ml (1 tbsp) chopped fresh tarragon
beaten egg to glaze**

Roll out two-thirds of the pastry and use to line a 23-cm (9-in) pie dish. Chop the onion. Melt the butter in a saucepan and fry the onion for 15 minutes. Stir in the flour and cook for 2 minutes. Gradually add the milk, bring to the boil, stirring, and cook for 1–2 minutes. Remove from the heat and season.

Meanwhile poach the fish in a little extra milk until tender. Remove the skin and bones. Chop the eggs and stir into the sauce with the fish and tarragon. Spoon the filling into the lined pie dish. Roll out the remaining pastry and use

to make a lid. Seal the edges well and trim. Use any pastry trimmings to decorate the top. Brush with the beaten egg and bake in the oven at 200°C (400°F) mark 6 for 40 minutes. *Serves 6*

Not suitable for freezing

Golden lamb and kidney puffs

**1 medium onion, skinned
2 lamb's kidneys, skinned and cored
25 g (1 oz) butter
100 g (4 oz) mushrooms, wiped
15 ml (1 tbsp) chopped fresh parsley
2.5 ml ($\frac{1}{2}$ level tsp) dried tarragon
salt and freshly ground pepper
45 ml (3 tbsp) red wine
30 ml (2 tbsp) vegetable oil
four 175-g (6-oz) lamb chump chops, trimmed
369-g (13-oz) packet frozen puff pastry, thawed
beaten egg to glaze**

Chop the onion and kidney. Melt the butter in a saucepan and cook the onion and kidney for 4 minutes. Chop the mushrooms finely and stir into the kidney mixture with the herbs, seasoning and wine. Cook for 2 minutes and leave to cool slightly. Meanwhile heat the oil in a frying pan and fry the chops for 3 minutes each side. Remove from the pan and cool slightly.

Divide the pastry into four and roll out to form squares. Spoon a little of the kidney mixture on to each of the pastry squares, place a chop on each and spoon over the remaining kidney mixture. Dampen the edges of the pastry and fold over to enclose the chops. Seal well, turn over and place on a baking tray. Brush with the beaten egg and bake in the oven at 220°C (425°F) mark 7 for 25 minutes until golden. *Serves 4*

To freeze Cool quickly, then pack individually in foil. To serve, leave at room temperature for 2–4 hours then reheat, covered, in the oven at 190°C (375°F) mark 5 for 30 minutes.

Creamy garlic stuffed chicken

1 large garlic clove, skinned
100 g (4 oz) cream cheese
15 ml (1 level tbsp) chopped fresh parsley
grated rind of $\frac{1}{2}$ a lemon
4 chicken breasts, skinned and beaten flat
25 g (1 oz) seasoned flour
2 eggs, beaten
175 g (6 oz) fresh white breadcrumbs
oil for deep frying

Chop the garlic then add the cream cheese, parsley and lemon rind and blend to form a purée. Roll the mixture in a piece of greaseproof paper or foil and put in the refrigerator until firm.

Divide the filling equally between the chicken breasts, folding them over and securing with wooden cocktail sticks. Coat in seasoned flour then in egg and breadcrumbs twice. Fry in deep fat or oil for about 8–10 minutes, until crisp and golden brown. Remove the cocktail sticks, leave to cool, then place in the refrigerator until cold. Serve with a salad.
Serves 4

To freeze Wrap individually in foil and place together in a polythene bag. To serve, allow to thaw overnight in the refrigerator.

Meat loaf

175 g (6 oz) streaky bacon, rinded
225 g (8 oz) lean cooked lamb
1 small onion, skinned
15 ml (1 level tbsp) tomato purée
10 ml (2 tsp) chopped fresh sage
43-g (1$\frac{1}{2}$-oz) packet bread sauce mix
150 ml ($\frac{1}{4}$ pint) milk
1 egg
15 ml (1 tbsp) red wine
salt and freshly ground pepper

Lightly oil a 450-g (1-lb) loaf tin and line with the bacon rashers. Mince the lamb and finely chop the onion and mix together with the tomato purée, sage and bread sauce mix. Beat

together the milk, egg, wine and seasoning. Pour into the meat mixture and mix well. Spoon into the lined loaf tin and press down. Cover with foil and bake in the oven at 200°C (400°F) mark 6 for 1–1$\frac{1}{4}$ hours. Turn out and serve in slices, hot or cold.
Serves 4

To freeze Line the loaf tin with foil before putting in the bacon and meat mixture, then cover and freeze. When frozen remove the loaf from the tin, wrap in foil and return to the freezer. To serve hot, unwrap the loaf and return to the tin while still frozen. Thaw overnight in a refrigerator, then cook as above. Alternatively freeze after cooking and turning out, wrapped in foil. To serve cold, thaw overnight in the refrigerator.

Lamb with cider and apples

15 g ($\frac{1}{2}$ oz) butter
4 lamb chump chops
1 medium onion, skinned
450 g (1 lb) cooking apples, peeled and cored
300 ml ($\frac{1}{2}$ pint) dry cider
30 ml (2 tbsp) chopped fresh parsley
salt and freshly ground pepper
15 ml (1 level tbsp) cornflour
60 ml (4 tbsp) double cream
chopped fresh parsley to garnish

Melt the butter in a frying pan and cook the chops for 10 minutes until brown on both sides. Chop the onion, add to the pan and cook for 5 minutes until soft. Chop the apples and stir into the chops and onion with the cider, parsley and seasoning. Cover and simmer gently for 15 minutes.

Blend the cornflour with a little water to make a smooth paste. Stir into the pan and bring to the boil, stirring continuously. Stir in the cream and reheat gently without boiling. Serve garnished with chopped parsley.
Serves 4

To freeze Cool quickly, omitting the cream and parsley, then pack in a rigid container.

Alternatively, line a small casserole with foil and put in the chops and sauce; freeze until firm, then remove from the casserole, wrap in foil and return to the freezer in a sealed polythene bag. To serve, remove the wrappings and reheat from frozen in a casserole in the oven at 190°C (375°F) mark 5 for about 1 hour; stir in the cream and garnish as above.

Chicken burgers with apple sauce

450 g (1 lb) cooked chicken
75 g (3 oz) flat mushrooms, wiped
2 medium onions, skinned
100 g (4 oz) fresh brown breadcrumbs
salt and freshly ground pepper
1 egg, beaten
flour for coating
fat or oil for shallow frying
15 g ($\frac{1}{2}$ oz) butter
450 g (1 lb) cooking apples, peeled and cored
300 ml ($\frac{1}{2}$ pint) chicken stock
25 g (1 oz) sultanas

For the burgers, chop the chicken, mushrooms and one onion and mix together with the breadcrumbs and seasoning. Bind together with the egg, divide into eight and shape into rounds. Coat the burgers in a little flour and fry for about 10 minutes on each side until golden brown. Drain on kitchen paper towel and keep warm.

For the sauce, melt the butter in a saucepan. Chop the remaining onion and cook in the butter for 5 minutes until soft. Chop the apples, add to the onion with the stock and simmer gently for about 10–15 minutes until the apple is soft. Blend the apple and onion mixture to form a purée and return to the saucepan. Add the sultanas and seasoning and reheat for 5 minutes. Serve the burgers coated with the sauce.
Serves 4

To freeze Make the chicken burgers but do not fry. Freeze with layers of greaseproof paper between each burger. Pack the sauce in a rigid container and freeze separately. To serve, fry the burgers from frozen for 12–15 minutes on each side. Reheat the sauce from frozen for 15–20 minutes.

Chilli con carne

350 g (12 oz) dried or 432-g (15$\frac{1}{4}$-oz) can red kidney beans, drained
700 g (1$\frac{1}{2}$ lb) lean stewing steak
1 large onion, skinned
1 medium carrot, peeled
2 sticks of celery, trimmed
15 ml (1 tbsp) vegetable oil
1 garlic clove, skinned and crushed
396-g (14-oz) can tomatoes
45 ml (3 level tbsp) tomato purée
15 ml (1 level tbsp) paprika
5 ml (1 level tsp) sugar
5–10 ml (1–2 level tsp) chilli powder
15 ml (1 tbsp) vinegar
salt and freshly ground pepper
30 ml (2 tbsp) red wine, optional

If using dried kidney beans, soak the beans overnight in cold water. Drain, then cook in boiling salted water for 45 minutes, or until tender. Rinse under cold water.

Mince the steak and chop the onion, carrot and celery. Fry the vegetables in the oil with the garlic for 5 minutes then add the meat and fry for a further 5 minutes. Add the tomatoes, tomato purée, paprika, sugar, chilli powder, vinegar, and seasoning and simmer gently for 30 minutes. Add the beans and the wine if used and cook for a further 10 minutes. Serve with a fresh green salad and hot French bread.
Serves 4–6

To freeze Omit the beans and cool quickly, then pack in a rigid container. To serve, reheat from frozen in a saucepan for about 20 minutes adding the beans about 10 minutes before the end of the cooking time.

Chicken and apricot casserole

Illustrated in colour facing page 48

175 g (6 oz) dried apricots
25 g (1 oz) butter
4 chicken portions, skinned
1 medium onion, skinned
50 g (2 oz) button mushrooms
salt and freshly ground pepper
25 g (1 oz) flour
150 ml ($\frac{1}{4}$ pint) chicken stock
300 ml ($\frac{1}{2}$ pint) dry white wine
chopped fresh parsley to garnish

Soak the apricots overnight in cold water. Drain and chop roughly, reserving a few whole apricots. Melt the butter in a large frying pan and cook the chicken portions on both sides for about 5 minutes until golden brown. Place in a casserole. Slice the onion and add to the pan with the mushrooms. Season and fry for 2 minutes. Add the flour and cook for 1 minute, then stir in the stock, wine and chopped apricots. Bring to the boil and pour over the chicken, adding the reserved apricots. Cover and cook in the oven at 180°C (350°F) mark 4 for 1$\frac{1}{2}$ hours. Garnish with chopped parsley.
Serves 4

To freeze Cool quickly, then pack in a rigid container. To serve, thaw overnight in the refrigerator, then reheat in the oven at 190°C (375°F) mark 5 for 30–40 minutes.

Mackerel parcels with mustard parsley butter

Herrings are a good alternative to mackerel for this dish.

175 g (6 oz) butter, softened
60 ml (4 level tbsp) made mustard
30 ml (2 tbsp) chopped fresh parsley
grated rind of 1 lemon
salt and freshly ground pepper
4 fresh mackerel, cleaned and heads removed
lemon wedges and parsley sprigs to garnish

Blend the butter, mustard, parsley, lemon rind and seasoning together. Shape pieces of foil, each 23 × 23 cm (9 × 9 in), into four boat shapes suitable for holding the fish. Spread a little of the savoury butter on the bottom of the foil. Fill the cavity of each fish with most of the remaining savoury butter, reserving just a little. Make three diagonal slits on each side of each fish.

Place each fish in a foil boat and top with the reserved butter. Cook under a hot grill for about 10–15 minutes, turning once during cooking. Serve in the boats to retain the juices. Garnish with lemon wedges and parsley sprigs.
Serves 4

To freeze Wrap in foil and freeze before cooking. To serve, thaw at room temperature for 3–4 hours then cook as above.

Potato-topped liver with leeks

350 g (12 oz) lamb's liver
25 g (1 oz) dripping
350 g (12 oz) leeks, trimmed and washed
100 g (4 oz) onions, skinned
30 ml (2 level tbsp) flour
300 ml ($\frac{1}{2}$ pint) beef stock
salt and freshly ground pepper
700 g (1$\frac{1}{2}$ lb) potatoes, peeled
30 ml (2 tbsp) milk
30 ml (2 tbsp) chopped fresh parsley
225 g (8 oz) tomatoes, skinned

Cut the liver into thin strips, discarding the skin and ducts. Heat the dripping in a saucepan and fry the liver for 3–5 minutes, until brown. Chop the leeks and onions and cook with the liver for 5–8 minutes until lightly browned. Stir in the flour and stock, bring to the boil and cook gently, stirring, until thickened. Season well, cover and simmer for about 15 minutes.

Meanwhile, chop the potatoes and cook in boiling salted water until tender. Mash with

the milk, adjust the seasoning and add the parsley. Place the liver mixture in a 1.7-litre (3-pint) ovenproof dish. Slice the tomatoes and arrange in a layer over the liver. Pipe or fork the potato mixture over the top. Either place the dish under a hot grill to brown, or bake in the oven at 200°C (400°F) mark 6 for 15–20 minutes.
Serves 4

Not suitable for freezing

Smoked cod gougère

450 g (1 lb) smoked cod
2 hard-boiled eggs
2 medium tomatoes, skinned
300 ml ($\frac{1}{2}$ pint) milk
25 g (1 oz) butter
25 g (1 oz) flour
salt and freshly ground pepper
15 ml (1 level tbsp) capers
15 ml (1 tbsp) lemon juice

For the choux paste
75 g (3 oz) butter
200 ml (7 fl oz) water
100 g (4 oz) plain flour, sifted
3 eggs, lightly beaten

For the topping
25 g (1 oz) fresh white breadcrumbs
15 g ($\frac{1}{2}$ oz) cheese

Place the fish in a saucepan. Cover with water and poach for 10 minutes. Drain and skin. Chop the fish, eggs and tomatoes roughly. Blend the milk, butter and flour together then pour into a saucepan and bring to the boil. Stir until the sauce thickens. Stir in the seasoning, capers and lemon juice and combine with the fish mixture.

For the choux paste, bring the butter and water to the boil. Add the flour all at once and beat well until it forms a ball. Cool slightly then gradually beat in the eggs. Using a 1-cm ($\frac{1}{2}$-in) plain nozzle, pipe the mixture around the sides of a lightly greased, shallow ovenproof

dish. Spoon the cod filling into the centre of the dish. Grate the cheese, combine with the breadcrumbs and sprinkle this topping over the fish. Bake in the oven at 220°C (425°F) mark 7 for 25 minutes. Serve immediately with a fresh green salad.
Serves 4

Not suitable for freezing

Trout with almond and lemon stuffing

Illustrated in colour facing page 48

2 medium trout, cleaned
15 g ($\frac{1}{2}$ oz) almonds
50 g (2 oz) fresh white breadcrumbs
15 ml (1 tbsp) chopped fresh parsley
grated rind and juice of $\frac{1}{2}$ small lemon
1 egg, beaten
150 ml ($\frac{1}{4}$ pint) white wine
2.5 ml ($\frac{1}{2}$ level tsp) dried tarragon
25 g (1 oz) flaked almonds
15 g ($\frac{1}{2}$ oz) butter
lemon wedges and watercress to garnish

Wash the trout and place in a shallow ovenproof dish. Roughly chop the almonds and mix with the breadcrumbs, parsley, lemon rind and juice and egg. Evenly fill the cavities of the fish with the stuffing.

Mix the white wine and dried tarragon together and pour over the fish. Fry the almonds in the butter until golden brown and spoon over the fish. Cover with foil and cook in the oven at 180°C (350°F) mark 4 for 25 minutes. Remove the foil and cook for a further 5 minutes. Garnish with lemon wedges and watercress and serve with boiled new potatoes and fresh green vegetables.
Serves 4

To freeze Wrap in foil before cooking. To serve, allow to thaw overnight in the refrigerator, then bake as above.

Mushroom mustard burgers

Illustrated in colour on the jacket

450 g (1 lb) lean beef
1 small onion, skinned
75 g (3 oz) mushrooms, wiped
40 g (1½ oz) fresh brown breadcrumbs
15 ml (1 level tbsp) made mustard
salt and freshly ground pepper
1 egg
30 ml (2 tbsp) cooking oil
onion slices to garnish

Mince the beef, chop the onion and mush-rooms and mix together with the bread-crumbs, mustard and seasoning. Bind together with the egg. Divide the mixture into eight and on a floured surface shape into 1-cm (½-in) thick rounds. Heat the oil in a large frying pan and fry the beef burgers for 4–5 minutes on each side, then remove to a serving dish and keep warm. Fry the onion slices for 2–3 minutes until golden brown and spoon over the burgers. Serve with mustard and tomato sauce (see below).
Serves 4

To freeze Prepare the burgers but do not fry. Freeze with layers of greaseproof paper be-tween each burger. To serve, fry from frozen for 6–8 minutes on each side and serve with onion slices as above.

Mustard and tomato sauce

½ small onion, skinned
396-g (14-oz) can tomatoes
15 ml (1 level tbsp) made mustard
5 ml (1 tsp) vinegar
30 ml (2 level tbsp) tomato purée
10 ml (2 tsp) sugar
salt and freshly ground pepper
knob of butter
15 ml (1 level tbsp) cornflour

Blend all the ingredients except the cornflour together to form a purée. Pour into a saucepan and bring to the boil. Simmer for 5 minutes.

Mix the cornflour with a little water and stir into the mustard and tomato sauce. Bring to the boil, stirring, and cook gently for 3–4 minutes.
Serves 4

To freeze Cool quickly and pack in a rigid container. To serve, reheat the frozen sauce gently in a saucepan.

Stuffed heart casserole

4 small lamb's hearts
2 small onions, skinned
25 g (1 oz) mushrooms
50 g (2 oz) fresh white breadcrumbs
30 ml (2 tbsp) melted butter
15 ml (1 tbsp) chopped fresh parsley
2.5 ml (½ level tsp) dried mixed herbs
salt and freshly ground pepper
30 ml (2 level tbsp) seasoned flour
25 g (1 oz) dripping
600 ml (1 pint) beef stock
4 sticks of celery, washed
2 medium carrots, peeled
15 ml (1 tbsp) dry sherry
30 ml (2 level tbsp) tomato purée

Wash the hearts, remove any tubes or gristle and wash again. For the stuffing, finely chop one onion and the mushrooms and combine with the breadcrumbs, butter, herbs and seasoning. Stuff the hearts and sew them firmly into their original shape with string.

Coat the hearts with seasoned flour and brown quickly in hot dripping. Place in a casserole with the stock. Cover and cook in the oven at 180°C (350°F) mark 4 for 2–2½ hours.

About 1 hour before the end of the cooking time chop the remaining onion, slice the celery and carrots and add to the casserole with the sherry and tomato purée. Transfer the hearts to a heated serving dish, removing the string, and keep warm. Purée the liquid and veg-etables to make a smooth sauce and pour this over the hearts.
Serves 4

To freeze Cool quickly, then pack into a rigid container. To serve, thaw overnight in the refrigerator, then cook in the oven at 190°C (375°F) mark 5 for about 30–40 minutes.

Beef and walnut pie

Illustrated in colour on the jacket

15 ml (1 tbsp) vegetable oil
450 g (1 lb) lean stewing steak
1 medium onion, skinned
15 ml (1 level tbsp) plain flour
1 garlic clove, skinned
50 g (2 oz) walnuts
50 g (2 oz) button mushrooms
30 ml (2 level tbsp) tomato purée
1 bay leaf
salt and freshly ground pepper
150 ml ($\frac{1}{4}$ pint) red wine
150 ml ($\frac{1}{4}$ pint) beef stock

For the pastry
50 g (2 oz) margarine
50 g (2 oz) lard
225 g (8 oz) plain flour
pinch of salt
25 g (1 oz) walnuts, finely chopped
beaten egg to glaze

Heat the oil in a large saucepan. Chop the beef and onion finely. Fry for 10 minutes until brown. Add the flour and mix well. Chop the garlic, walnuts and mushrooms and add to the beef and onion mixture in the pan with the tomato purée, bay leaf, seasoning, wine and stock. Mix well, cover the pan and simmer for 30 minutes. Remove the bay leaf and cool.

To make the pastry, mix the fat into the flour and salt to resemble breadcrumbs. Stir in the walnuts and mix in enough cold water to make a firm dough.

Roll out two-thirds of the pastry and use to line an oval 900 ml (1$\frac{1}{2}$ pint) pie dish. Fill the dish with the meat mixture, dampen the edges and cover with the remaining pastry. Seal well and use the pastry trimmings to decorate the top.

Brush with beaten egg and bake in the oven at 190°C (375°F) mark 5 for 30 minutes. Serve immediately.
Serves 4

To freeze Wrap in foil before baking. To serve, unwrap and bake from frozen in the oven at 180°C (350°F) mark 4 for about 1–1$\frac{1}{4}$ hours. After about 30 minutes, cover the pastry with foil to prevent it burning.

Peppers with lamb and rice stuffing

4 medium green or red peppers
1 small onion, skinned
1 garlic clove, skinned
100 g (4 oz) streaky bacon, rinded
15 ml (1 tbsp) vegetable oil
225 g (8 oz) cold cooked lamb
15 ml (1 tbsp) Worcestershire sauce
15 ml (1 level tbsp) tomato purée
salt and freshly ground pepper
75 g (3 oz) long grain rice, cooked
50 g (2 oz) cheese
tomato sauce (see page 44)

Cut a slice off the top of each pepper and remove the core and seeds. Blanch the peppers in boiling salted water for 5 minutes. Drain and put in an ovenproof dish. Chop the onion, garlic and bacon and mix together. Heat the oil in a saucepan and fry the bacon mixture for 5 minutes. Mince the lamb and add to the bacon with the Worcestershire sauce, tomato purée, seasoning and rice. Cook for a further 2–3 minutes then spoon the stuffing into the peppers. Grate the cheese and sprinkle over the top. Surround with the tomato sauce.

Cover with foil and bake in the oven at 190°C (375°F) mark 5 for 30 minutes, or until the peppers are tender.
Serves 4

To freeze Cover the dish with foil before baking. To serve, thaw for 4 hours at room temperature, then cook as above.

Tomato sauce

1 medium onion, skinned
25 g (1 oz) butter
25 g (1 oz) flour
150 ml ($\frac{1}{4}$ pint) chicken stock
396-g (14-oz) can tomatoes
5 ml (1 level tsp) sugar
5 ml (1 level tsp) dried mixed herbs
15 ml (1 level tbsp) tomato purée
salt and freshly ground pepper
15 ml (1 tbsp) red wine, optional

Chop the onion. In a saucepan fry the onion in the butter for about 10 minutes until soft. Blend with the remaining ingredients until smooth. Return to the saucepan, bring to the boil and cook for 3–4 minutes, stirring continuously. This sauce is particularly good with stuffed peppers (page 43) but it is also delicious served with other vegetable dishes.
Serves 4

To freeze Cool quickly and pack in a rigid container. To serve, reheat frozen sauce gently in a saucepan for about 20 minutes.

Pork fillet with sage stuffing

two 350-g (12-oz) pork fillets
25 g (1 oz) seasoned flour
1 small onion, skinned
225 g (8 oz) streaky bacon, rinded
50 g (2 oz) butter
100 g (4 oz) fresh white breadcrumbs
30 ml (2 tbsp) chopped fresh sage
30 ml (2 tbsp) chopped fresh parsley
salt and freshly ground pepper
grated rind and juice of 1 small lemon
1 egg, beaten
100 g (4 oz) button mushrooms, wiped
150 ml ($\frac{1}{4}$ pint) dry white wine
150 ml ($\frac{1}{4}$ pint) chicken stock
60 ml (4 tbsp) soured cream

Make a horizontal cut along the length of the fillets, two thirds of the way through. Open out the fillets, cover with greaseproof paper and

beat out to an even thickness. Toss in seasoned flour. To make the stuffing, finely chop the onion and bacon and cook in 25 g (1 oz) butter for 5 minutes. Mix in the breadcrumbs, sage, parsley, seasoning, lemon rind and juice and egg. Spread the stuffing over the fillets, then roll them up and tie neatly with string.

Melt the remaining butter in a frying pan and fry the fillet rolls for 10 minutes until evenly brown. Place in a casserole with the mushrooms, wine, stock and seasoning. Cook in the oven at 180°C (350°F) mark 4 for about 1 hour.

Remove the fillets to a warm serving dish and remove the strings. Stir the soured cream into the casserole then pour over the meat. Divide each fillet into three to serve.
Serves 6

To freeze Cool quickly and pack into a rigid container. To serve, leave at room temperature for 4–6 hours then reheat, covered, in the oven at 190°C (375°F) mark 5 for 45–50 minutes.

Spicy oven-baked chicken

1.6-kg ($3\frac{1}{2}$-lb) roasting chicken
25 g (1 oz) butter
1 small onion, skinned
1 medium carrot, peeled
2 sticks of celery, trimmed
1 small eating apple, peeled and cored
1 medium tomato, skinned
1 garlic clove, skinned
15 ml (1 level tbsp) concentrated
  curry sauce
30 ml (2 level tbsp) flour
300 ml ($\frac{1}{2}$ pint) chicken stock
10 ml (2 tsp) lemon juice
30 ml (2 tbsp) cream
salt and freshly ground pepper
chopped fresh parsley to garnish

Roast the chicken in the oven at 200°C (400°F) mark 6 for 1$\frac{1}{2}$ hours. Pour off the juices and reserve. Allow the chicken to cool slightly.

Melt the butter in a saucepan. Chop the onion, carrot, celery, apple, tomato and garlic and fry slowly for 10 minutes. Stir in the curry sauce and flour. Gradually add the stock and bring to the boil, stirring. Simmer for 15 minutes, stirring occasionally. Blend the sauce to form a purée. Add the lemon juice, cream and seasoning to taste.

Remove the skin from the cooked chicken and cut the bird into large portions. Place in an ovenproof dish. Skim the surface fat from the chicken juices and add the juices to the sauce. Reheat the sauce and pour over the chicken. Cover and cook in the oven at 190°C (375°F) mark 5 for about 20 minutes. Garnish with chopped parsley.
Serves 4

To freeze Cool quickly, then pack in a rigid container. To serve, leave in the refrigerator overnight until thoroughly thawed, then reheat in the oven at 190°C (375°F) mark 5 for about 45 minutes and serve garnished with parsley as above.

Chicken layer puff

two 369-g (13-oz) packets frozen puff pastry, thawed
15 ml (1 tbsp) olive oil
1 medium onion, skinned
50 g (2 oz) button mushrooms, wiped
450 g (1 lb) cold cooked chicken
25 g (1 oz) peanuts
15 ml (1 tbsp) chopped fresh parsley
pinch of ground nutmeg
salt and freshly ground pepper
175 g (6 oz) butter, melted

Divide the pastry into 12 pieces and roll each out very thinly to about 25.5-cm (10-in) squares, layering them up with greaseproof paper in between. Heat the oil in a saucepan. Finely chop the onion and mushrooms and fry for 5–6 minutes. Finely chop the chicken and nuts and stir into the onion with the parsley and seasonings. Cook for a further 2–3 minutes.

Place a layer of pastry on a floured baking sheet and brush with melted butter, repeat with another layer, then spoon over some of the chicken mixture. Repeat with two layers of pastry brushed with butter and some filling until all the filling is used. End with pastry and brush liberally with melted butter.

Bake in the oven at 190°C (375°F) mark 5 for 45 minutes or until crisp and golden brown. Serve immediately.
Serves 6

Not suitable for freezing

Sausage pie

1 large onion, skinned
2 large tomatoes, skinned
1 eating apple, peeled and cored
450 g (1 lb) sausagemeat
5 ml (1 level tsp) chopped fresh herbs
30 ml (2 level tbsp) tomato purée
salt and freshly ground pepper
175 g (6 oz) shortcrust pastry
  (see page 57)
beaten egg to glaze

Finely chop the onion, tomato and apple and mix with the sausagemeat, herbs, tomato purée and seasoning. Place in a 700-ml (1¼-pint) oval pie dish. Roll out the pastry on a lightly floured surface and use to cover the pie. Seal and flute the edge and use any pastry trimmings to decorate the top. Make a hole in the centre. Brush with beaten egg and bake in the oven at 200°C (400°F) mark 6 for 30–35 minutes, then reduce the temperature to 170°C (325°F) mark 3 and bake for a further 15 minutes.
Serves 4–6

To freeze Wrap and freeze before baking. To serve, thaw overnight in the refrigerator, then bake as above.

Chop vegetables quickly and easily with a food processor

Chicken and lemon croquettes

225 g (8 oz) cooked chicken
1 small onion, skinned
50 g (2 oz) Cheddar cheese
30 ml (2 tbsp) chopped fresh parsley
grated rind and juice of 1 lemon
25 g (1 oz) butter
25 g (1 oz) flour
150 ml ($\frac{1}{4}$ pint) chicken stock
salt and freshly ground pepper
flour for coating
1 egg, beaten
75 g (3 oz) fresh brown breadcrumbs
oil for deep frying
sprigs of watercress and lemon slices
   to garnish

Mince the chicken and onion and grate the cheese, and mix together with the parsley, lemon rind and juice. Blend the butter, flour and stock together until smooth, then pour into a saucepan, bring to the boil and stir until thickened. Season well. Add the sauce to the chicken mixture and mix well.

Cool the mixture and place in a covered bowl in a refrigerator for 1 hour to chill. Divide the mixture into eight, shape into rolls and coat in flour. Dip the croquettes in the egg and roll them in the breadcrumbs. Heat the oil to 190°C (375°F) mark 5 and fry a few of the croquettes at a time for 5 minutes until golden brown. Drain on kitchen paper towel and keep warm until the remaining croquettes are cooked. Garnish with watercress and lemon.
Serves 4

To freeze Open freeze before frying on a lined baking tray. When frozen, pack into a rigid container or polythene bag. To serve, thaw in a refrigerator for 2 hours, then cook and serve as above.

Spaghetti alla bolognese

1 medium carrot, peeled
1 medium onion, skinned
1 garlic clove, skinned
30 ml (2 tbsp) vegetable oil
450 g (1 lb) lean stewing steak
225 g (8 oz) streaky bacon, rinded
100 g (4 oz) button mushrooms
30 ml (2 level tbsp) flour
226-g (8-oz) can tomatoes
300 ml ($\frac{1}{2}$ pint) beef stock
60 ml (4 level tbsp) tomato purée
2.5 ml ($\frac{1}{2}$ level tsp) dried oregano
salt and freshly ground pepper
30 ml (2 tbsp) red wine
225 g (8 oz) spaghetti
grated Parmesan cheese to serve

Finely chop the carrot, onion and garlic. Heat the oil in a large saucepan and fry the chopped vegetables for about 5 minutes. Mince the meat and bacon and add to the pan. Fry for a further 10 minutes until lightly browned.

Roughly chop the mushrooms and stir into the meat mixture with the flour. Blend the tomatoes to a purée and add to the pan with the stock, tomato purée, oregano, seasoning and wine. Bring to the boil, then simmer for 50–60 minutes.

Cook the spaghetti in boiling salted water for 12–15 minutes. Drain well. Serve with the

sauce poured over and topped with Parmesan cheese.
Serves 4

To freeze Cool the bolognese sauce then pack in a rigid container. To serve, reheat the sauce from frozen for about 30 minutes in a saucepan. Cook the spaghetti and serve as above.

Pork, veal and orange one-crust pie

700 g (1½ lb) shoulder of pork
350 g (12 oz) stewing veal
25 g (1 oz) seasoned flour
60 ml (4 tbsp) oil
1 large onion, skinned
1 large carrot, peeled
grated rind and juice of 1 large orange
15 ml (1 level tbsp) cornflour
salt and freshly ground pepper
175 g (6 oz) shortcrust pastry (see page 57)
milk to glaze

Remove any fat from the meat and finely chop or mince. Toss in the seasoned flour and keep any surplus flour. Heat 30 ml (2 tbsp) oil in saucepan and fry the meat for 10 minutes until it starts to brown. Place in a 1.4 litre (2½ pint) oval pie dish. Slice the onion and carrot, add the remaining oil to the pan and fry the vegetables for 1–2 minutes, without browning. Add to the meat. Make the orange juice up to 300 ml (½ pint) with water. Blend together the remaining seasoned flour, cornflour and orange rind with the orange juice mixture until smooth. Pour into the pan and bring to the boil, stirring all the time until thickened. Season, pour over the filling and cool.

Roll out the pastry and use to cover the pie dish. Seal and flute the edge and decorate with pastry leaves made from the trimmings. Make a hole in the centre and brush with milk. Bake in the oven at 200°C (400°F) mark 6 for 30 minutes, then reduce the heat to 170°C (325°F) mark 3 and bake for a further 15 minutes.
Serves 4–6

To freeze Wrap in foil and freeze before baking. To serve, allow to thaw overnight in the refrigerator, then bake as above.

Somerset veal

4 veal escalopes
30 ml (2 tbsp) vegetable oil
1 medium onion, skinned
1 cooking apple, peeled and cored
100 g (4 oz) button mushrooms
15 ml (1 level tbsp) plain flour
150 ml (¼ pint) dry cider
150 ml (¼ pint) chicken stock
1 eating apple, cored
25 g (1 oz) butter
30 ml (2 tbsp) single cream
salt and freshly ground pepper
15 ml (1 tbsp) chopped fresh parsley to garnish

Trim the veal and fry in the oil in a large saucepan until lightly browned on both sides. Remove from the pan. Finely chop the onion and apple and fry with the mushrooms for 5 minutes. Stir in the flour and gradually add the cider and stock. Bring to the boil, stirring until thickened. Return the veal to the pan, cover and cook for 15–20 minutes until tender. Meanwhile slice the eating apple and fry in the butter until soft.

Remove the veal to a serving dish and keep warm, then blend the remaining sauce until smooth. Return the sauce to the pan and add the single cream. Season to taste. Cook gently until heated through, without allowing the sauce to boil, and pour a little over the veal. Serve the remaining sauce separately in a jug. Garnish with the fried apple slices and chopped parsley.
Serves 4

To freeze Pack in a rigid container, omitting the garnish. To serve, reheat from frozen in a shallow casserole in the oven at 190°C (375°F) mark 5 for 40 minutes. Garnish as above.

Steak and kidney pudding

225 g (8 oz) self raising flour
100 g (4 oz) shredded suet
2.5 ml ($\frac{1}{2}$ level tsp) salt
550 g ($1\frac{1}{4}$ lb) lean stewing steak
100 g (4 oz) lamb's kidney, skinned and
  cored
30 ml (2 level tbsp) seasoned flour
1 small onion, skinned
100 g (4 oz) button mushrooms
15 ml (1 tbsp) chopped fresh parsley
15 ml (1 level tbsp) tomato purée
30 ml (2 tbsp) red wine
30 ml (2 tbsp) beef stock

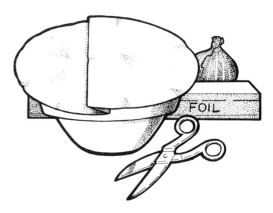

Covering the pudding before cooking

Mix together the flour, suet and salt. Add enough cold water to give a light, elastic dough and knead very lightly until smooth. Roll out to about 0.5 cm ($\frac{1}{4}$ in) thick, into a circle large enough to line a 1.1-litre (2-pint) pudding basin. Cut out a quarter segment and line the bowl with the remainder.

Finely chop the steak and kidney and mix with the flour. Finely chop the onion and mushrooms and mix into the chopped meat with the parsley and tomato purée. Place the mixture in the lined bowl. Pour over the wine and stock. Roll out the remaining pastry to make a lid, damping the edges with water to seal them together.

Cover with pleated, greased, greaseproof paper and foil and secure with string. Cook the

pudding in a steamer or over a saucepan of boiling water for about 4 hours, topping up the water when necessary. Remove the cover and turn out of the bowl to serve.
Serves 4–6

Not suitable for freezing

Veal and lemon pie

700 g ($1\frac{1}{2}$ lb) stewing veal
225 g (8 oz) streaky bacon, rinded
25 g (1 oz) seasoned flour
45 ml (3 tbsp) oil
1 medium onion, skinned
1 cooking apple, peeled
1 medium carrot, peeled
salt and freshly ground pepper
grated rind and juice of 1 lemon
10 ml (2 level tsp) cornflour
215-g ($7\frac{1}{2}$-oz) packet frozen puff pastry,
  thawed
beaten egg to glaze

Remove any fat from the meat and chop it. Chop the bacon separately. Toss the veal in the seasoned flour and keep any surplus flour. Heat 30 ml (2 tbsp) oil in a large frying pan and fry the meat and bacon half at a time for 10 minutes, until beginning to brown. Remove from the pan. Roughly chop the onion and apple and grate the carrot. Add the remaining

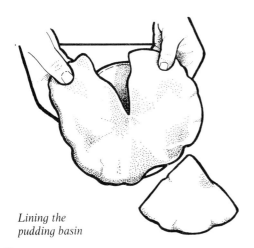

Lining the pudding basin

48

Chicken and apricot casserole (page 40),
Trout with almond and lemon stuffing (page 41)

oil to the pan and fry the vegetables and apple for 1–2 minutes without allowing them to brown. Place the meat and vegetables in a 1.4-litre (2½-pint) shallow greased pie dish. Season well.

Blend the lemon rind and juice with the corn-flour and remaining flour, then make up to 450 ml (¾ pint) with water. Pour into the pan and bring to the boil, stirring until thickened. Pour over the filling and cool.

Roll out the pastry and use to cover the pie dish. Knock up and flute the edges. Make a hole in the centre and decorate with pastry leaves made from the trimmings. Brush with beaten egg. Bake in the oven at 200°C (400°F) mark 6 for 30 minutes, then cover loosely with foil and reduce the oven temperature to 170°C (325°F) mark 3 and bake for a further 30 minutes.
Serves 4

To freeze Cool the filling and pack in a rigid container. To serve, thaw at room temperature for 3–4 hours, then cover with the pastry, brush with beaten egg and bake as above.

Bacon toad in the hole

225 g (8 oz) plain flour
2 eggs
salt and freshly ground pepper
450 ml (¾ pint) milk
150 ml (¼ pint) water
325 g (12 oz) lean hock or collar bacon
50 g (2 oz) fresh white breadcrumbs
15 ml (1 level tbsp) tomato purée
2.5 ml (½ tsp) Worcestershire sauce
45 ml (3 tbsp) chopped fresh parsley
25 g (1 oz) lard or dripping

Blend together the flour, eggs, seasoning, milk and water until smooth. Finely mince the bacon and mix with the breadcrumbs, tomato purée, Worcestershire sauce and parsley. Add pepper but no salt. Form the mixture into eight equal-sized balls.

Heat the fat in a shallow 23-cm (9-in) roasting tin. Place the bacon balls, evenly spaced, in the tin. Bake in the oven at 200°C (400°F) mark 6 for 15 minutes. Loosen the bacon balls but leave in place. Pour the batter into the hot fat around the bacon and return to the oven for about 45 minutes until well risen and golden.
Serves 4

Not suitable for freezing

Lasagne verdi

1 large onion, skinned
450 g (1 lb) lean stewing steak
15 ml (1 tbsp) oil
396-g (14-oz) can tomatoes
pinch of dried mixed herbs
salt and freshly ground pepper
25 g (1 oz) butter
25 g (1 oz) flour
300 ml (½ pint) milk
25 g (1 oz) Cheddar cheese
8 sheets of lasagne verdi, cooked

Roughly chop the onion. Finely chop or mince the meat. Heat the oil in a pan and fry the onion for 5 minutes until soft. Add the meat and fry for a further 5 minutes until brown. Add the tomatoes, herbs and seasoning. Cook gently for 20 minutes.

Meanwhile make the sauce. Blend the butter, flour, milk and seasoning together until smooth. Pour into a saucepan and slowly bring to the boil, stirring all the time until thickened. Put half the meat in the bottom of an oven-proof dish. Arrange 4 sheets of lasagne on top. Repeat these two layers and pour the sauce over the top. Grate the cheese and sprinkle over the dish, then bake in the oven at 180°C (350°F) mark 4 for 30 minutes.
Serves 4

To freeze Cover the dish with foil and freeze before baking. To serve, thaw overnight in the refrigerator, then bake as above.

Country pork pie (page 51)

Lamb stuffed aubergines with cider sauce

4 medium aubergines
1 large onion, skinned
1 garlic clove, skinned
15 ml (1 tbsp) vegetable oil
1 small apple, peeled and cored
450 g (1 lb) cold cooked lamb
salt and freshly ground pepper
2.5 ml ($\frac{1}{2}$ tsp) chopped fresh mint
600 ml (1 pint) beef stock

For the sauce
40 g (1$\frac{1}{2}$ oz) butter
40 g (1$\frac{1}{2}$ oz) flour
150 ml ($\frac{1}{4}$ pint) milk
300 ml ($\frac{1}{2}$ pint) dry cider
75 g (3 oz) Red Leicester cheese

Cut the aubergines in half and score the cut surfaces well. Sprinkle liberally with salt and put aside for at least 30 minutes. Rinse under water, then pat dry. Place on a baking sheet and bake in the oven at 200°C (400°F) mark 6 for 30 minutes or until soft. Scoop out and finely chop the flesh.

Chop the onion and garlic. Heat the oil in a large saucepan and fry the onion and garlic for 5 minutes. Chop the apple and mince the lamb, and stir into the saucepan with the aubergine flesh. Cook for a further 5 minutes. Stir in the seasoning, mint and stock. Spoon the stuffing into the aubergine shells and place in a shallow ovenproof dish.

For the sauce, blend the butter, flour, milk, cider and seasoning together until smooth. Pour into a saucepan and bring to the boil, stirring until thickened. Pour the sauce over the aubergines. Grate the cheese and sprinkle over the top. Bake in the oven at 200°C (400°F) mark 6 for 20 minutes until golden brown.
Serves 4

To freeze Cool quickly and cover the dish with foil. To serve, place the frozen covered aubergines in the oven at 180°C (350°F) mark 4 for 40 minutes until heated through.

Lamb stuffed aubergines with cider sauce

Crispy topped chicken with mushrooms

8 chicken portions
1 carrot, peeled
1 onion, skinned
1.25 ml ($\frac{1}{4}$ tsp) dried tarragon
6 peppercorns
salt
100 g (4 oz) button mushrooms, wiped
50 g (2 oz) butter
25 g (1 oz) plain flour
150 ml ($\frac{1}{4}$ pint) double cream
15 ml (1 level tbsp) chopped fresh parsley
75 g (3 oz) fresh white breadcrumbs
75 g (3 oz) Red Leicester cheese

Put the chicken in a saucepan with the carrot, onion, tarragon, peppercorns, 5 ml (1 level tsp) salt and enough water to cover. Bring to the boil and cook for 1–2 hours, or until tender. Drain the chicken and strain and reserve 300 ml ($\frac{1}{2}$ pint) of the stock.

Cook the mushrooms in half the butter for 5 minutes and blend to form a purée. Blend the remaining butter, flour and reserved stock together until smooth. Pour into a saucepan and bring to the boil, stirring all the time until thickened. Stir in the mushroom purée and gradually add the cream and parsley. Heat gently without boiling and season to taste.

Arrange the chicken in a flameproof dish and pour over the sauce. Grate the cheese, mix with the breadcrumbs and sprinkle over the top. Place under a hot grill until crisp and golden brown.
Serves 4

To freeze Freeze without the topping. To serve, thaw overnight in the refrigerator, then add the cheese and breadcrumbs and reheat in the oven at 200°C (400°F) mark 6 for 30 minutes.

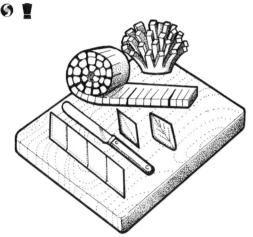

Making a tassel and leaves to decorate a pie

Country pork pie

Illustrated in colour facing page 49

525 g (18 oz) shortcrust pastry (see page 57 and treble the recipe)
175 g (6 oz) streaky bacon rashers, rinded
700 g (1½ lb) lean pork
1 large onion, skinned
350 g (12 oz) sausagemeat
5 ml (1 level tsp) dried sage
10 ml (2 tsp) Worcestershire sauce
salt and freshly ground pepper
4 hard-boiled eggs
beaten egg to glaze

Roll out two-thirds of the pastry and use to line a 20.5-cm (8-in) round loose-bottomed cake tin. Mince the bacon and pork, and chop the onion, and mix together with the sausagemeat, sage, Worcestershire sauce and seasoning. Place half the pork mixture in the lined tin. Arrange the eggs over the top and cover with the remaining pork mixture.

Roll out the remaining pastry and make a lid to cover the pie. Dampen the edge and seal and flute. Make a slit in the centre and use any pastry trimmings to decorate the top. Brush with egg and bake in the oven at 200°C (400°F) mark 6 for 1½ hours, covering the lid with foil after 30 minutes to prevent burning. Leave in the tin until cold.
Serves 8–10

Not suitable for freezing

Apricot stuffed lamb

1 medium onion, skinned
4 rashers of streaky bacon, rinded
25 g (1 oz) dried apricots
75 g (3 oz) fresh brown breadcrumbs
10 ml (2 tsp) chopped fresh thyme
salt and freshly ground pepper
1 egg
1.4-kg (3-lb) leg of lamb, boned
watercress to garnish

Chop the onion, bacon and apricots and mix with the breadcrumbs, thyme and seasoning. Bind together with the egg and mix well. Fill the lamb cavity with the stuffing and sew up neatly with string, or secure with skewers. Weigh the joint and roast in the oven for 25 minutes per 450 g (1 lb), plus 25 minutes, at 180°C (350°F) mark 4. Garnish with watercress.
Serves 4–6

To freeze Wrap in foil and freeze before roasting. To serve, thaw in the refrigerator overnight, then cook as above.

Tuna scallops

450 g (1 lb) potatoes, peeled
75 g (3 oz) butter
2 hard-boiled eggs
198-g (7-oz) can tuna fish, drained
25 g (1 oz) butter
25 g (1 oz) flour
salt and freshly ground pepper
300 ml ($\frac{1}{2}$ pint) milk
grated rind and juice of $\frac{1}{2}$ lemon
75 g (3 oz) Cheddar cheese
25 g (1 oz) fresh white breadcrumbs
chopped fresh parsley to garnish

Cook the potatoes in boiling salted water until soft. Drain and beat well with the butter until smooth. Fork or pipe the potato into a border in six scallop shells or individual ovenproof dishes. Roughly chop the egg, mix with the tuna and put into the centre of each 'nest'.

Blend together the butter, flour, seasoning and milk and pour into a saucepan. Bring to the boil, stirring continuously until thickened. Add the lemon rind and juice. Grate the cheese and add 25 g (1 oz) to the sauce. Pour the sauce over the tuna and egg. Sprinkle with the remaining cheese and the breadcrumbs and brown under a hot grill. Garnish with parsley.
Serves 6

Not suitable for freezing

Shepherd's pie

700 g (1$\frac{1}{2}$ lb) potatoes, peeled
450 g (1 lb) cold cooked lamb
1 large onion, skinned
1 large carrot, peeled
50 g (2 oz) butter or margarine
15 ml (1 level tbsp) flour
226-g (8-oz) can tomatoes
2.5 ml ($\frac{1}{2}$ level tsp) dried mixed herbs
2.5 ml ($\frac{1}{2}$ tsp) Worcestershire sauce
salt and freshly ground pepper
30 ml (2 tbsp) milk

Cook the potatoes in boiling salted water until tender. Mince the lamb. Chop the onion and carrot.

Melt 25 g (1 oz) of the fat in a saucepan and fry the onion and carrot for about 10 minutes until browned. Blend together the flour, tomatoes and their juice, herbs, Worcestershire sauce, salt and pepper. Pour into the pan, bring to the boil and simmer for 5 minutes. Stir in the meat, then turn into an ovenproof dish.

Drain the potatoes thoroughly and beat with the milk and remaining fat until smooth. Spread the potato evenly over the meat and mark the top with a fork. Bake in the oven at 190°C (375°F) mark 5 for 30 minutes until golden brown.
Serves 4

To freeze Cool the unbaked pie and cover. To serve, thaw at room temperature for 4–5 hours, then bake as above.

Minced lamb with soured cream and peppers

450 g (1 lb) boned shoulder of lamb
1 large onion, skinned
1 green pepper, halved and seeded
1 red pepper, halved and seeded
50 g (2 oz) butter
225 g (8 oz) button mushrooms
1 chicken stock cube
45 ml (3 level tbsp) plain flour
150 ml ($\frac{1}{4}$ pint) milk
salt and freshly ground pepper
150 ml ($\frac{1}{4}$ pint) soured cream
chopped fresh parsley to garnish

Coarsely mince the lamb. Chop the onion and slice the peppers. Melt 25 g (1 oz) butter in a saucepan and gently fry the onion and peppers for 5 minutes. Add the minced lamb and mushrooms and cook for a further 3 minutes, stirring.

Dissolve the stock cube in 150 ml ($\frac{1}{4}$ pint) boiling water and add to the pan. Cover and simmer for 30 minutes. Drain and reserve the liquid from the meat.

Blend the remaining butter, flour, milk and reserved liquid together until smooth. Pour into a saucepan and bring to the boil, stirring. Cook gently until the sauce thickens. Stir the meat and vegetables into the sauce, bring to the boil and adjust the seasoning. Turn into a warmed serving dish, swirl in the soured cream and sprinkle with parsley.
Serves 4

To freeze Cool, then pack in a rigid container, omitting the cream and parsley. To serve, thaw overnight in the refrigerator, then reheat in a saucepan for about 20 minutes, adding the cream and parsley as above.

minutes until the bananas are soft but not mushy.

Meanwhile, for the sauce, blend the butter, flour, stock, lemon juice and seasoning until smooth. Pour into a pan and bring to the boil, stirring all the time until the sauce thickens. Place the chicken and bananas on a heated serving dish and pour over the sauce. Garnish with watercress and lemon slices.
Serves 4

To freeze Cool, then pack in a rigid container omitting the garnish. To serve, thaw overnight in the refrigerator, then reheat gently in a saucepan for about 20 minutes. Garnish as above.

Sautéed chicken and banana with lemon sauce

1.4-kg (3-lb) roasting chicken
seasoned flour
100 g (4 oz) streaky bacon rashers
50 g (2 oz) butter
3 bananas
30 ml (2 tbsp) lemon juice
watercress and lemon slices to garnish

For the sauce
25 g (1 oz) butter
25 g (1 oz) flour
600 ml (1 pint) chicken stock
30 ml (2 tbsp) lemon juice
salt and freshly ground pepper

Wipe the chicken and joint into eight pieces, discarding the rib carcass. Toss each piece well in seasoned flour. Remove the rind and roughly chop the bacon, then fry in a large saucepan until the fat runs. Add the butter, then gently fry the chicken for 5–10 minutes until golden brown on all sides. Cover and cook, turning occasionally, for about 30 minutes until thoroughly cooked and tender.

Slice the bananas and add to the chicken. Pour the lemon juice over and cook for about 3

53

Lunches, Suppers and Snacks

Herby pork sausages

225 g (8 oz) lean belly of pork
1 large onion, skinned
175 g (6 oz) fresh suet
50 g (2 oz) fresh white breadcrumbs
2.5 ml ($\frac{1}{2}$ level tsp) dried rosemary
2.5 ml ($\frac{1}{2}$ level tsp) dried thyme
pinch of grated nutmeg
grated rind of 1 lemon
salt and freshly ground pepper
1 egg
dripping for frying

Finely mince the pork and onion and grate the suet. Mix together with the breadcrumbs, herbs, nutmeg, lemon rind and seasoning. Beat the egg into the mixture. With floured hands, shape the mixture into 8 sausage shapes. Heat the dripping in a frying pan and fry the sausages for 20 minutes until golden brown on all sides.
Makes 8

To freeze Open freeze raw sausages, then pack into a rigid container or wrap in foil. To serve, thaw overnight in a refrigerator then fry as above.

Apple and beef pasta

25 g (1 oz) butter
1 medium onion, skinned
700 g (1$\frac{1}{2}$ lb) lean stewing steak
40 g (1$\frac{1}{2}$ oz) flour
600 ml (1 pint) beef stock
15 ml (1 level tbsp) tomato purée
450 g (1 lb) cooking apples, peeled and cored
225 g (8 oz) tomatoes, skinned
15 ml (1 tbsp) Worcestershire sauce
2.5 ml ($\frac{1}{2}$ level tsp) dried basil
1.25 ml ($\frac{1}{4}$ level tsp) grated nutmeg
salt and freshly ground pepper
225 g (8 oz) pasta shells
chopped fresh parsley to garnish

Melt the butter in a large saucepan. Chop the onion and mince the beef and cook in the butter for 10 minutes until brown. Stir in the flour and cook for 2 minutes. Add the stock and tomato purée and bring to the boil, stirring. Chop the apples and tomatoes and stir into the pan with the Worcestershire sauce, basil, nutmeg and seasoning. Cover the pan and simmer gently for 25 minutes.

Meanwhile cook the pasta shells in boiling salted water for about 12 minutes, then drain. Add the cooked pasta shells to the beef mixture and heat gently for a further 5 minutes. Serve garnished with chopped parsley.
Serves 4

To freeze Cool and pack into a rigid container. To serve, thaw overnight in the refrigerator. Heat gently in a saucepan and garnish as above.

Beef balls in barbecue sauce

350 g (12 oz) lean stewing steak
100 g (4 oz) bacon
15 ml (1 tbsp) chopped fresh mixed herbs
salt and pepper
vegetable oil for frying

For the sauce
1 large onion, skinned
50 g (2 oz) butter
5 ml (1 level tsp) tomato purée
30 ml (2 tbsp) white vinegar
30 ml (2 level tbsp) demerara sugar
10 ml (2 level tsp) dry mustard
30 ml (2 tbsp) Worcestershire sauce

Mince together the stewing steak and bacon. Mix in the herbs and seasoning. Shape into 24 small balls with floured hands. Chill for 30 minutes.

Meanwhile make the sauce. Chop the onion finely. Melt the butter and fry the onion for 5 minutes until soft. Stir in the tomato purée and continue to cook for a further 2 minutes. Blend together the remaining ingredients with 150 ml ($\frac{1}{4}$ pint) water. Stir into the onion and simmer for 10 minutes.

Lightly oil the base of a frying pan. Fry the meat balls for 7 minutes until cooked, turning frequently. Drain on kitchen paper towel. Pile meat balls into a warm serving dish and serve with the sauce.
Serves 4

To freeze Cool the meat balls and sauce quickly, then pack together in a foil container. To serve, reheat the frozen meat balls, covered, in the oven at 190°C (375°F) mark 5 for 30 minutes until heated through.

Flan provençal

Illustrated in colour facing page 33

450 g (1 lb) onions, skinned
2 garlic cloves, skinned
90 ml (6 tbsp) vegetable oil
225 g (8 oz) tomatoes, skinned
30 ml (2 level tbsp) tomato purée
2.5 ml ($\frac{1}{2}$ level tsp) Provence herbs
salt and freshly ground pepper
anchovy fillets and black olives to garnish

For the shortcrust pastry (makes 175 g [6 oz])
25 g (1 oz) butter
25 g (1 oz) lard
100 g (4 oz) plain flour
pinch of salt

For the pastry, cut the fats into pieces and add to the flour and salt. Mix until the mixture resembles fine breadcrumbs. Add about 30 ml (2 tbsp) cold water and mix until it forms a smooth dough. Wrap and leave to chill in a refrigerator or cool place for 15 minutes. Roll out the pastry and use to line a 20.5-cm (8-in) plain flan ring. Bake blind in the oven at 200°C (400°F) mark 6 for 20 minutes.

Meanwhile, for the filling, finely slice the onions and crush the garlic and fry in the oil in a large saucepan for 10 minutes until very soft but not coloured. Slice the tomatoes, add to the pan and continue cooking until the liquid has evaporated. Stir in the tomato

purée, herbs and seasoning. Turn the mixture into the flan case. Brush with a little oil and cook in the oven at 200°C (400°F) mark 6 for 20 minutes. Garnish with a lattice of anchovy fillets and the olives. Serve hot or cold.
Serves 6

To freeze Cool quickly, open freeze and wrap. To serve, leave wrapped at room temperature for 4 hours. To serve hot, place on a baking tray, covered with foil, and reheat at 180°C (350°F) mark 4 for 30 minutes.

Baked anchovy rolls

When celery is not available, add a few chopped walnuts instead.

50-g (1$\frac{3}{4}$-oz) can anchovy fillets
milk to soak
3 sticks celery heart
100 g (4 oz) butter, softened
freshly ground pepper
15 ml (1 tbsp) lemon juice
8 large bridge rolls

Drain the anchovies and cover with a little milk and leave to soak for 20 minutes. Strain off the milk and blend the anchovies until smooth. Chop the celery finely and beat into the anchovies with the butter, pepper and lemon juice. Slice diagonally through each roll, making three cuts and leaving the bottom crust intact. Spread the anchovy butter between the slices and place the rolls side by side on a large sheet of foil. Wrap the foil loosely around them and place on a baking tray. Bake in the oven at 220°C (425°F) mark 7 for 15 minutes. Serve piping hot.
Makes 8

To freeze Wrap in foil as above, then freeze before baking. To serve, place the frozen rolls loosely covered with the foil on a baking tray. Heat in the oven at 230°C (450°F) mark 8 for 15 minutes.

Tagliatelle with salami cream sauce

275 g (10 oz) tagliatelle verdi
1 small onion, skinned
1 garlic clove, skinned
15 ml (1 tbsp) vegetable oil
225 g (8 oz) salami
30 ml (2 tbsp) chopped fresh parsley
freshly ground pepper
150 ml ($\frac{1}{4}$ pint) soured cream
60 ml (4 tbsp) milk
chopped fresh parsley to garnish

Cook the tagliatelle in a pan of boiling salted water for about 10 minutes until just tender. Drain and keep warm. Meanwhile chop the onion and garlic. Heat the oil in a large saucepan and cook the onion and garlic gently for 5 minutes until soft.
Chop the salami and add to the onion with the parsley and seasoning. Mix well and cook gently for 5 minutes. Stir in the soured cream and milk and heat very gently without boiling for a few minutes. Add the cooked tagliatelle to the sauce and turn into a warm serving dish. Garnish with chopped parsley.
Serves 2–3

Not suitable for freezing

Olive cheese fingers

75 g (3 oz) butter
225 g (8 oz) plain savoury biscuits
75 g (3 oz) stuffed olives
1 small onion, skinned
100 g (4 oz) Cheddar cheese
salt and freshly ground pepper
1 egg
150 ml ($\frac{1}{4}$ pint) milk

Melt the butter in a large saucepan. Crush the biscuits and mix into the butter. Reserve eight olives and chop the rest. Finely chop the onion and grate the cheese. Mix together the chopped olives, onion and cheese with the seasoning, egg and milk. Stir into the crumb

mixture and press into a 25.5 × 15-cm (10 × 6-in) shallow tin. Slice the remaining olives and sprinkle over the top. Bake in the oven at 190°C (375°F) mark 5 for 20 minutes. Leave to stand for 5 minutes then cut into sixteen fingers. Serve hot or cold.
Makes 16

To freeze Cool, remove from the tin and wrap in foil or pack into a rigid container. To serve hot, place on a baking tray and reheat at 180°C (350°F) mark 4 for 20 minutes until warmed through. To serve cold, leave at room temperature for 5 hours.

Avocado dip

2 medium avocados
30 ml (2 tbsp) lemon juice
50 g (2 oz) cream cheese
75 ml (5 level tbsp) natural yogurt
1 small garlic clove, skinned and crushed
salt and freshly ground pepper
2.5 ml ($\frac{1}{2}$ tsp) Worcestershire sauce
chopped fresh parsley to garnish

Halve the avocados, remove the stones and scoop out the flesh. Blend the flesh with all the remaining ingredients until smooth. Spoon into a serving dish and garnish with the parsley. Chill for 30 minutes. Serve with fingers of warm toast or prepared raw vegetables. Eat the same day.
Serves 6

Not suitable for freezing

Cheese and bacon shorties

100 g (4 oz) streaky bacon, rinded
175 g (6 oz) plain flour
2.5 ml ($\frac{1}{2}$ level tsp) dry mustard
salt and freshly ground pepper
1.25 ml ($\frac{1}{4}$ level tsp) paprika
100 g (4 oz) butter
100 g (4 oz) Cheddar cheese

Grill the bacon until crisp, cool, then crumble finely. Mix together the flour, mustard, seasoning and paprika. Mix in the butter until the mixture resembles breadcrumbs. Grate the cheese. Stir in the bacon and cheese, and mix together to form a soft dough. Press the mixture into a 28 × 18-cm (11 × 7-in) oblong tin. Level the surface and bake in the oven at 180°C (350°F) mark 4 for about 35 minutes until golden brown. Allow to cool slightly, then cut into fingers and ease out of the tin.
Makes about 24

To freeze Wrap in foil or pack into a rigid container. To serve, place frozen shorties on a baking tray and reheat in the oven at 180°C (350°F) mark 4 for 15 minutes.

Flaky pâté puffs

50 g (2 oz) salted mixed nuts
100 g (4 oz) soft liver pâté
15 ml (1 level tbsp) made mustard
freshly ground pepper
312-g (12-oz) packet frozen puff pastry, thawed
1 beaten egg to glaze

Chop the nuts finely. Beat the pâté, mustard, half the nuts and pepper well together. Roll out the pastry thinly and cut out 20 rounds using a 9-cm ($3\frac{1}{2}$-in) plain cutter. Fold and re-roll the trimmings as necessary. Place a little pâté mixture on each round and brush the edges of the pastry with beaten egg. Fold each round in half to form a half moon shape and seal the edges well. Place the puffs on baking tray, brush with egg and sprinkle with the remaining nuts. Bake in the oven at 220°C (425°F) mark 7 for about 15 minutes.
Makes 20

To freeze Cool, then wrap or pack in a rigid container. To serve, place the frozen puffs on a baking sheet and bake in the oven at 190°C (375°F) mark 5 for 10–15 minutes until heated through.

Cheese and walnut loaf

Cheshire cheese is a good alternative to Red Leicester.

225 g (8 oz) self raising flour
2.5 ml ($\frac{1}{2}$ level tsp) dry mustard
pinch of salt
50 g (2 oz) hard margarine
25 g (1 oz) walnuts
75 g (3 oz) Red Leicester cheese
150 ml ($\frac{1}{4}$ pint) milk
1 egg

Sift together the flour, mustard and salt. Mix in the margarine until the mixture resembles fine breadcrumbs. Finely chop the walnuts and grate the cheese. Mix in and bind together with the milk and egg to form a soft dough. Spoon the mixture into a greased, base-lined 900-ml ($1\frac{1}{2}$-pint) loaf tin. Bake in the oven at 180°C (350°F) mark 4 for 45 minutes. Turn out and cool on a wire rack. Serve sliced, while still slightly warm.
Serves 6

To freeze Cool quickly then wrap. To serve, leave at room temperature for 4 hours, or place the frozen loaf loosely wrapped in foil in the oven at 180°C (350°F) mark 4 for 45 minutes to serve warm.

Peanut butter

275 g (10 oz) salted peanuts
50 g (2 oz) butter, softened

Blend 225 g (8 oz) peanuts and the butter together until smooth. Add the remaining peanuts and roughly chop. This gives an extra crunch to the butter. If a smooth butter is required blend all the nuts together. Serve with crusty bread.

Not suitable for freezing. Store covered in the refrigerator for up to 3 weeks

Jansson's temptation

This is a traditional Swedish dish.

350 g (12 oz) potatoes, peeled
1 large onion, skinned
50-g (1¾-oz) can anchovy fillets
75 g (3 oz) butter
40 g (1½ oz) fresh white breadcrumbs
150 ml (¼ pint) milk
100 g (4 oz) Cheddar cheese

Thinly slice the potatoes and onions and finely chop the anchovies with their oil. Mix well together. Use half the butter to grease an ovenproof dish and spoon in the potato mixture. Melt the remaining butter in a pan and lightly fry the breadcrumbs for a few minutes. Sprinkle them over the potatoes. Cover the dish with foil and bake in the oven at 200°C (400°F) mark 6 for 35 minutes.

Remove the foil and pour the milk into the dish at one side. Grate the cheese and sprinkle over the top, then return to the oven, uncovered, for 20–30 minutes until the potatoes are cooked and the crumbs golden brown. Serve hot.
Serves 2

To freeze Cool quickly then cover. To serve, reheat from frozen in the oven at 170°C (325°F) mark 3 for 45 minutes until warmed through. Remove the cover and increase the heat to 200°C (400°F) mark 6 for 10–15 minutes.

Golden haddock soufflé

75 g (3 oz) Red Leicester cheese
25 g (1 oz) butter
25 g (1 oz) flour
150 ml (¼ pint) milk
salt and freshly ground pepper
3 eggs, separated
100 g (4 oz) smoked haddock, cooked
    and flaked
30 ml (2 tbsp) chopped fresh chives

Grate the cheese. Lightly grease an 18-cm (7-in) soufflé dish. Blend together the butter, flour and milk. Pour into a saucepan and, whisking all the time, slowly bring to the boil. Cook for 1–2 minutes until thickened. Cool slightly and stir in the seasoning, egg yolks, fish, cheese and chives. Stiffly whisk the egg whites and fold into the fish mixture, then spoon into the soufflé dish. Bake in the oven at 200°C (400°F) mark 6 for 35 minutes until well risen and golden brown. Serve immediately.
Serves 4

Not suitable for freezing

Stilton pancakes

For the batter
100 g (4 oz) flour
300 ml (½ pint) milk
1 egg
pinch of salt
oil for frying

For the filling
350 g (12 oz) cold cooked chicken
1 medium onion, skinned
salt and freshly ground pepper

For the sauce
25 g (1 oz) butter
25 g (1 oz) flour
300 ml (½ pint) milk
salt and freshly ground pepper
100 g (4 oz) Stilton cheese

Mix or blend the batter ingredients (not oil). Heat a little oil in a small frying pan. Pour a little of the batter mixture into the pan, turning it round to cover the base thinly. Cook quickly until golden brown underneath, turn with a palette knife or by tossing and cook the second side until golden. Turn out on to kitchen paper towel and repeat to make eight pancakes.

Finely chop the chicken and onion and mix with the seasoning. Place in the centre of each pancake, then roll them up and place in a lightly buttered ovenproof dish.

Blend together the sauce ingredients and pour into a saucepan. Whisking all the time, bring to the boil over a medium heat. Cook for 1–2 minutes until thickened, then pour over the pancakes and put in the oven at 190°C (375°F) mark 5 for 20 minutes until the pancakes are heated through and the sauce golden.
Makes 8

To freeze Pack the pancakes and sauce separately in rigid containers before baking. To serve, thaw at room temperature for 2 hours and reheat in the oven at 200°C (400°F) mark 6 for 15 minutes.

Seafood soufflé omelette

25 g (1 oz) butter
25 g (1 oz) peeled prawns
25 g (1 oz) peeled shrimps
15 ml (1 tbsp) lemon juice
15 ml (1 tbsp) chopped fresh parsley
2 eggs
salt and freshly ground pepper

Make the filling by melting half the butter in a saucepan and cooking the prawns, shrimps, lemon juice and parsley together for 5 minutes.

Meanwhile separate the eggs and place the yolks and whites in different bowls. Whisk the yolks until creamy and add seasoning. Beat in 30 ml (2 tbsp) water. Whisk the egg whites until stiff but not dry. Heat the remaining butter in a frying pan over a low heat. Carefully fold the egg whites into the egg yolk

mixture, taking care not to over mix. Pour the egg mixture into the pan and cook over a medium heat until the omelette is golden brown on the underside.

Place the frying pan under the grill until the omelette is browned on top. Run a spatula gently around the edge of the omelette to loosen it and make a mark across the middle. Add the filling to one half and fold the omelette over. Turn out on to a warm plate and serve immediately.
Serves 1

Not suitable for freezing

Leeks au gratin

4 medium leeks, trimmed
100 g (4 oz) streaky bacon, rinded
25 g (1 oz) butter
45 ml (3 level tbsp) flour
300 ml ($\frac{1}{2}$ pint) milk
salt and freshly ground pepper
2.5 ml ($\frac{1}{2}$ level tsp) dry mustard
100 g (4 oz) Cheddar cheese
25 g (1 oz) shelled walnuts
50 g (2 oz) fresh white breadcrumbs

Slice and wash the leeks and cook in boiling salted water for 10–15 minutes. Drain well. Meanwhile chop the bacon and fry in its own fat for about 10 minutes until crisp. Blend together the butter, flour, milk, seasoning and mustard until smooth. Pour the sauce into a saucepan and bring to the boil, whisking all the time until it thickens. Cook for 1–2 minutes. Grate the cheese and stir half into the sauce.

Spoon the leeks into a lightly greased oven-proof dish and pour the sauce over the leeks. Sprinkle the bacon on top. Chop the nuts and mix with the remaining cheese and bread-crumbs. Sprinkle over the dish and place under a hot grill until crisp and golden brown.
Serves 4

Not suitable for freezing

Tuna and mushroom egg mornay

8 hard-boiled eggs
25 g (1 oz) mushrooms, wiped
99-g (3½-oz) can tuna fish, drained
30 ml (2 level tbsp) mayonnaise
grated rind of ½ a lemon
10 ml (2 tsp) lemon juice
5 ml (1 level tsp) mushroom ketchup
salt and freshly ground pepper
40 g (1½ oz) butter
40 g (1½ oz) flour
450 ml (¾ pint) milk
100 g (4 oz) Cheddar cheese

Cut the eggs in half lengthways and remove the yolks. Chop the yolks and mushrooms finely, then blend in the tuna fish, mayonnaise, lemon rind and juice, mushroom ketchup and seasoning. Fill the eggs with the fish mixture and press back together. Place in an ovenproof dish.

Blend together the butter, flour, milk and cheese. Pour into a saucepan and bring to the boil, whisking all the time over a moderate heat. Cook for 1–2 minutes until thickened. Pour the sauce over the eggs and bake in the oven at 180°C (350°F) mark 4 for 15 minutes.
Serves 4

Not suitable for freezing

Hummus

Illustrated in colour facing page 32

A traditional recipe from the Middle East served with warm pitta bread.

225 g (8 oz) chick peas
salt and freshly ground black pepper
90 ml (6 tbsp) lemon juice
90 ml (6 tbsp) olive oil
1–2 garlic cloves, skinned and crushed
15 ml (1 level tbsp) sesame seeds
pinch of cumin seeds
chopped fresh parsley to garnish

Wash the peas, cover with cold water and leave to soak for 12 hours or overnight. Drain, place

in a saucepan and cover with cold salted water. Bring to the boil and simmer gently for 2 hours or until tender. Add more boiling water if necessary to keep the peas covered with water throughout the cooking time. Drain and reserve a few whole peas for garnish.

Gradually purée the remaining peas with all the lemon juice until smooth. Beat in the oil and garlic. Add the sesame seeds and cumin and season to taste. Spoon into a serving dish and sprinkle over the reserved chick peas and parsley.
Serves 8

To freeze Pack in a rigid container, omitting the garnish. To serve, thaw overnight at room temperature. Beat again if necessary and garnish as above.

Stuffed mushroom fritters

450 g (1 lb) large button mushrooms
225 g (8 oz) liver sausage or smooth pâté
50 g (2 oz) butter, melted
1 garlic clove, skinned and crushed
30 ml (2 tbsp) chopped fresh parsley
salt and freshly ground pepper
flour for coating
2 eggs, beaten
225 g (8 oz) fresh white breadcrumbs
oil for deep frying
parsley sprigs to garnish

Remove the stalks from the mushrooms and chop the stalks finely.

Beat together the liver sausage and butter until soft. Stir in the garlic, parsley, seasoning and chopped mushroom stalks and use this mixture to stuff the mushroom caps.

Coat the mushrooms in flour, dip in the beaten egg and roll in the breadcrumbs. Heat the oil to 180°C (350°F) and fry the mushrooms, a few at a time, for 4 minutes until golden brown. Drain on kitchen paper towel. Place in a warmed serving dish and garnish with parsley springs.
Serves 4

marinade and put under a hot grill for 15–20 minutes, turning once and brushing with the marinade. Serve garnished with the parsley. *Serves 4*

To freeze Pack in a rigid container before cooking. To serve, thaw in a refrigerator for 3 hours and cook as above.

Mackerel pasta

175 g (6 oz) pasta shells
700 g (1½ lb) cooked mackerel, skinned
and boned
½ cucumber
1 large red pepper, seeded
30 ml (2 level tbsp) horseradish cream
90 ml (6 tbsp) single cream
30 ml (2 tbsp) lemon juice
chopped fresh parsley to garnish

For the mayonnaise
2 egg yolks
salt and freshly ground pepper
5 ml (1 level tsp) dry mustard
300 ml (½ pint) vegetable oil
30 ml (2 tbsp) wine vinegar

Cook the pasta shells in boiling salted water for about 12 minutes, then drain, rinse under cold water and drain again. Flake the mackerel into a large bowl. Dice the cucumber and slice the pepper and add to the fish.

To make the mayonnaise, blend together the egg yolks, seasoning and mustard. Very slowly blend in the oil a little at a time until the mayonnaise begins to thicken. Blend in the vinegar.

Add the horseradish cream, cream and lemon juice to the mayonnaise. Fold the mayonnaise into the fish and add the pasta. Spoon into a serving dish and garnish.
Serves 6

Not suitable for freezing

To freeze Cool quickly, open freeze, then wrap. To serve, place frozen mushrooms on a baking tray and reheat in the oven at 200°C (400°F) mark 6 for 15 minutes until crisp.

Grilled marinated cod cutlets

4 large cod cutlets
45 ml (3 tbsp) vegetable oil
30 ml (2 tbsp) lemon juice
30 ml (2 tbsp) soy sauce
10 ml (2 tsp) Worcestershire sauce
2.5 ml (½ level tsp) dry mustard
1 garlic clove, skinned
1 small onion, skinned and chopped
2.5 ml (½ level tsp) salt
2.5 ml (½ level tsp) paprika
150 ml (¼ pint) chicken stock
chopped fresh parsley to garnish

Place the cod cutlets in a shallow dish. Blend together all the remaining ingredients except the parsley. Pour over the fish, cover and leave in a refrigerator for 2 hours, turning the cutlets after one hour. Place in a grill pan with the

Hawaiian chicken soufflé

4 eggs, separated
2.5 ml (½ level tsp) salt
30 ml (2 tbsp) lemon juice
225 g (8 oz) cooked chicken
298-g (10½-oz) can condensed
** chicken soup**
340-g (12-oz) can crushed pineapple
25 g (1 oz) flaked almonds, toasted
freshly ground pepper
25 g (1 oz) powdered gelatine
shredded lettuce

Prepare a 900-ml (1½-pint) soufflé dish with a band of greaseproof paper around the top. Place a 450-g (1-lb) jam jar, with a weight inside it, in the centre. Place the egg yolks, salt and lemon juice in a basin over hot water. Whisk until really thick and creamy. Finely chop the chicken and stir in with the soup, pineapple and almonds. Season well with pepper.

In a small bowl sprinkle the gelatine into 60 ml (4 tbsp) water. Stand the bowl over a pan of hot water and stir until dissolved. Leave to cool and stir into the cool chicken mixture. Stiffly whisk the egg whites and fold these in. Spoon into the soufflé dish, around the jam jar, and chill until set. To serve, pour hot water into the jam jar and quickly twist it out. Remove the paper collar. Fill the centre cavity with shredded lettuce.
Serves 6

Preparing the soufflé dish

To freeze Open freeze before garnishing with lettuce, then cover. To serve, unwrap and thaw in a refrigerator for 4 hours. Garnish as above.

Salmon herb loaf with hollandaise sauce

The hollandaise sauce is very quick and easy to make in a blender or food processor.

75 g (3 oz) fresh white breadcrumbs
150 ml (¼ pint) milk
213-g (7½-oz) can red salmon
2 eggs
15 ml (1 tbsp) lemon juice
grated rind of 1 lemon
15 ml (1 level tbsp) tomato purée
15 ml (1 tbsp) chopped fresh parsley
salt and freshly ground pepper

For the hollandaise sauce
1 egg
15 ml (1 tbsp) lemon juice
salt and freshly ground pepper
50 g (2 oz) butter
15 ml (1 tbsp) boiling water

Grease a 450-g (1-lb) loaf tin. Blend together all the loaf ingredients until smooth. Spoon into the prepared tin. Bake in the oven at 180°C (350°F) mark 4 for 45 minutes until set. Leave the loaf to cool in the tin, then turn out and slice.

To make the sauce, blend the egg, lemon juice and seasoning together. Melt the butter in a saucepan and gradually pour into the egg mixture, blending well. Then blend in the water. Pour the sauce over the loaf and serve.
Serves 4

To freeze Cool the loaf quickly and turn out of tin. Open freeze, then wrap. To serve, thaw in the refrigerator overnight. The sauce is not suitable for freezing.

Mushrooms with creamy noodles

100 g (4 oz) wholemeal noodles
salt and freshly ground pepper
15 g ($\frac{1}{2}$ oz) butter
1 medium onion, skinned
450 g (1 lb) button mushrooms, wiped
30 ml (2 tbsp) dry white wine
30 ml (2 tbsp) double cream
50 g (2 oz) Gruyère cheese
30 ml (2 level tbsp) fresh white breadcrumbs

Cook the noodles in boiling salted water for about 12 minutes until tender. Drain thoroughly. Meanwhile, melt the butter in a saucepan, slice the onion and fry for 5 minutes. Slice the mushrooms and stir into the onion with the wine and seasoning. Cook for 10 minutes until the mushrooms are tender.

Stir the noodles and cream into the mushroom mixture and continue cooking for 2 minutes. Spoon the mushroom mixture into a warmed flameproof dish. Grate the cheese and sprinkle on top with the breadcrumbs. Cook under a hot grill for 3 minutes until golden brown and crisp.
Serves 2

Not suitable for freezing

Vegetables, Salads and Preserves

Hot potato salad

450 g (1 lb) potatoes, peeled
2 rashers of streaky bacon, rinded
1 small onion, skinned
15 ml (1 level tbsp) flour
5 ml (1 level tsp) sugar
2.5 ml ($\frac{1}{2}$ level tsp) salt
1.25 ml ($\frac{1}{4}$ tsp) paprika
15 ml (1 tbsp) wine vinegar
1 hard-boiled egg
chopped fresh parsley to garnish

Slice the potatoes and cook in boiling salted water for 10–15 minutes until just tender. Meanwhile chop the bacon and onion and fry together for 10 minutes until golden brown. Stir in the flour, sugar, salt, paprika, vinegar and 150 ml ($\frac{1}{4}$ pint) water. Bring to the boil, stirring continuously, and cook for 2 minutes.

Drain the potatoes and add to the bacon mixture. Continue cooking for 10 minutes, stirring occasionally, until the flavours are well blended. Chop the egg and stir in. Turn into a warmed serving dish and sprinkle with parsley.
Serves 4

Not suitable for freezing

Spiced swedes

1 medium onion, skinned
450 g (1 lb) swede, peeled
600 ml (1 pint) chicken stock
25 g (1 oz) butter
25 g (1 oz) flour
1.25 ml ($\frac{1}{4}$ level tsp) grated nutmeg
salt and freshly ground pepper
chopped fresh parsley to garnish

Slice the onion and swede and cook together in the stock for 25 minutes until tender. Drain, reserving 300 ml ($\frac{1}{2}$ pint) of the stock. Place the swede and onion in a dish, cover and keep warm.

Blend together the stock, butter, flour, nutmeg and seasoning. Pour into a saucepan and bring

to the boil, whisking all the time until it thickens. Cook for 1–2 minutes. Pour the sauce over the swede and sprinkle with parsley.
Serves 4

To freeze Cool quickly then cover, omitting the garnish. To serve, thaw at room temperature for 2 hours. Reheat, covered, in the oven at 170°C (325°F) mark 3 for 35–40 minutes, garnishing as above.

Dill cabbage sauté

75 g (3 oz) butter
1 medium onion, skinned
900 g (2 lb) white cabbage
150 ml ($\frac{1}{4}$ pint) dry white wine
2.5–5 ml ($\frac{1}{2}$–1 level tsp) dill seeds
salt and freshly ground pepper

Melt the butter in a large saucepan, chop the onion finely and cook for 5 minutes until soft but not coloured. Shred the cabbage finely, add to the onion and sauté for 3–4 minutes. Stir in the white wine and dill seeds. Season well. Cover and simmer gently for 5–10 minutes until the cabbage is just tender.
Serves 4–6

Not suitable for freezing

Ratatouille

1 large onion, skinned
1 green pepper, seeded
1 large aubergine
4 large tomatoes, skinned
225 g (8 oz) courgettes
1 garlic clove, skinned
30 ml (2 tbsp) vegetable oil
396-g (14-oz) can tomatoes
salt and freshly ground pepper
chopped fresh parsley to garnish

Slice the onion, pepper, aubergine, tomatoes and courgettes. Finely chop the garlic. Heat

the oil in a large saucepan and add the onion and garlic. Fry for 5 minutes until soft. Add the pepper and aubergine and fry for a further 5 minutes. Add the tomatoes, courgettes, can of tomatoes and seasoning. Cover and simmer gently for 35–45 minutes until tender, stirring occasionally. Spoon into a warm serving dish and sprinkle with parsley.
Serves 4–6

To freeze Cool quickly, then pack into a rigid container, omitting the garnish. To serve, reheat, covered, in the oven at 180°C (350°F) mark 4 for 30 minutes and garnish as above.

Salad Niçoise

This classic French salad also makes a delicious sandwich filling between a split French loaf.

450 g (1 lb) tomatoes, skinned
$\frac{1}{2}$ small bunch of radishes, trimmed
**   and washed**
1 small green pepper, seeded
1 medium onion, skinned
$\frac{1}{2}$ cucumber, washed
50-g ($1\frac{3}{4}$-oz) can anchovy fillets, drained
12 black olives
15 ml (1 tbsp) chopped fresh parsley

For the dressing
45 ml (3 tbsp) wine vinegar
90 ml (6 tbsp) vegetable oil
2.5 ml ($\frac{1}{2}$ level tsp) made mustard
salt and freshly ground pepper

Cut the tomatoes into wedges and place in a large bowl. Slice the radishes, pepper and onion and add to the tomatoes. Roughly chop the cucumber and anchovy fillets and stir into the salad with the olives and parsley. Blend together the dressing ingredients, pour over the salad and toss well.
Serves 4

Not suitable for freezing

Cauliflower nut salad

1 medium cauliflower
2 hard-boiled eggs
50 g (2 oz) shelled walnuts
30 ml (2 tbsp) chopped fresh mixed herbs
150 ml ($\frac{1}{4}$ pint) vegetable oil
60 ml (4 tbsp) vinegar
pinch of dry mustard
salt and freshly ground pepper

Cut the cauliflower into small florets and wash well. Chop the eggs finely and the nuts roughly and add to the cauliflower with the herbs. Blend together the remaining ingredients and pour over the salad. Cover and leave for 3 hours before serving.
Serves 6–8

Not suitable for freezing

Marinated mushrooms

They can be served as a dinner party starter or as a salad.

1 medium onion, skinned
1 garlic clove, skinned
450 g (1 lb) button mushrooms, wiped
45 ml (3 tbsp) wine vinegar
90 ml (6 tbsp) vegetable oil
pinch of dry mustard
pinch of caster sugar
salt and freshly ground pepper
30 ml (2 tbsp) chopped fresh parsley

Finely chop the onion and garlic. Slice the mushrooms thickly and add to the onion and garlic. Blend together the vinegar, oil, mustard, sugar, seasoning and half the parsley. Pour the marinade over the mushrooms, cover and leave for 4 hours in a refrigerator. Sprinkle with the remaining parsley and serve.
Serves 4

Not suitable for freezing

Dijon potatoes

900 g (2 lb) potatoes, peeled
2 large onions, skinned
30 ml (2 tbsp) chopped fresh chives
30 ml (2 level tbsp) Dijon mustard
300 ml ($\frac{1}{2}$ pint) chicken stock
salt and freshly ground black pepper
25 g (1 oz) butter, melted

Slice the potatoes and onion thinly and arrange in alternate layers in a casserole dish, sprinkling each layer with the chives and ending with a potato layer. Blend together the mustard, stock and seasoning and pour over the potatoes. Brush the melted butter over the top, cover and bake in the oven at 180°C (350°F) mark 4 for 2 hours. Remove the cover 30 minutes before the end of the cooking time to brown the top.
Serves 6

To freeze Cool quickly then cover. To serve, thaw at room temperature for 3–4 hours and reheat in the oven at 200°C (400°F) mark 6 for 40 minutes.

Bacon spinach salad

225 g (8 oz) fresh young spinach
8 rashers of streaky bacon
45 ml (3 tbsp) vegetable oil
1 garlic clove, skinned and crushed
25 g (1 oz) fresh brown breadcrumbs
15 ml (1 tbsp) lemon juice
2.5 ml ($\frac{1}{2}$ level tsp) made mustard
salt and freshly ground pepper

Wash the spinach and remove any tough stems. Drain well and shred. Remove the rinds and roughly chop the bacon. Fry for 15 minutes until golden brown and drain on kitchen paper towel. Add 15 ml (1 tbsp) oil to the pan and fry the garlic and breadcrumbs together until crisp and golden.

Mix together the spinach, bacon and breadcrumbs. Blend together the remaining oil, lemon juice, mustard and seasoning. Pour over

the salad and toss well. Spoon into a serving bowl.
Serves 4

Not suitable for freezing

Lettuce and cucumber with lemon dressing

1 medium crisp lettuce, washed
$\frac{1}{2}$ cucumber, washed

For the dressing
grated rind and juice of 1 large lemon
90 ml (6 tbsp) vegetable oil
30 ml (2 tbsp) natural yogurt
30 ml (2 tbsp) chopped fresh mint

Shred the lettuce and slice the cucumber. Blend together the dressing ingredients until smooth. Pour the dressing over the salad and toss well. Chill before serving.
Serves 4

Not suitable for freezing

Lancashire summer salad

1 lettuce, washed
1 bunch radishes, trimmed and washed
1 cucumber, peeled
1 head chicory, trimmed and washed
350 g (12 oz) Lancashire cheese
watercress to garnish

For the dressing
30 ml (2 tbsp) vinegar
60 ml (4 tbsp) vegetable oil
2.5 ml ($\frac{1}{2}$ level tsp) dry mustard
salt and freshly ground pepper

Shred the lettuce and place in a large bowl. Slice the radishes, cucumber and chicory finely and dice the cheese. Mix into the lettuce. Blend together the dressing ingredients and pour over the salad. Toss well. Spoon into a serving

bowl and garnish with sprigs of watercress.
Serves 4

Not suitable for freezing

Lancashire summer salad

Cucumber pickle

3 large cucumbers, washed
4 large onions, skinned
45 ml (3 level tbsp) salt
450 ml ($\frac{3}{4}$ pint) white vinegar
150 g (5 oz) sugar
10 ml (2 level tsp) mustard seeds

Slice the cucumber and onion and place in a
large bowl with the salt. Leave for 1 hour then
drain and rinse. Heat the vinegar, sugar and
mustard seeds gently in a saucepan, stirring to
dissolve the sugar, and cook for 3 minutes.
Pack the vegetables into jars and add enough
hot vinegar mixture to cover. Seal immediately.
Makes about 2.3 kg (5 lb).

Store in a cool, dry place

Lemon marmalade

1.4 kg (3 lb) lemons
3.4 litres (6 pints) water
2.7 kg (6 lb) sugar

Halve the lemons and squeeze out the juice.
Cut each 'cap' in half with a sharp knife and
remove the membrane with some of the pith.
Put the membrane, pith and pips in a muslin
bag. Slice the peel and put the peel, juice, water
and muslin bag into a saucepan. Bring to the
boil and cook gently for about 2 hours until
the peel squashes easily between finger and
thumb.

Remove the muslin bag, squeezing the liquid
into the pan. Add the sugar and stir until
dissolved, then boil quickly until setting point
is reached. Allow to cool for about 15 minutes,
then stir gently before potting and covering in
the usual way.
Makes about 4.5 kg (10 lb).

Store in a cool, dry place

Cranberry and apple jam

700 g ($1\frac{1}{2}$ lb) cooking apples, peeled
   and cored
700 g ($1\frac{1}{2}$ lb) cranberries
300 ml ($\frac{1}{2}$ pint) water
1.5 kg (3 lb) sugar

Slice the apples and place in a saucepan with
the cranberries and water. Simmer gently for
about 15 minutes or until the fruit is tender.
Add the sugar, stir until dissolved and bring to
the boil. Boil rapidly for about 10 minutes or
until setting point is reached. Pot and cover in
the usual way.
Makes about 2.3 kg (5 lb).

Store in a cool, dry place

Celery and apple salad

1 head of celery, trimmed
50 g (2 oz) walnuts
3 red eating apples, cored

For the dressing
60 ml (4 tbsp) corn oil
30 ml (2 tbsp) wine vinegar
5 ml (1 level tsp) made mustard
2.5 ml ($\frac{1}{2}$ level tsp) caster sugar
10 ml (2 level tsp) chopped onion
10 ml (2 tsp) chopped fresh parsley
freshly ground black pepper

Blend together all the dressing ingredients. Chill for 30 minutes.

Roughly chop the celery and walnuts and dice the apples. Mix together in a large bowl. Pour over enough of the chilled dressing to moisten and toss well.
Serves 6

Not suitable for freezing

Jerusalem artichokes with mustard sauce

450 g (1 lb) Jerusalem artichokes
30 ml (2 tbsp) lemon juice
450 g (1 lb) firm ripe tomatoes, skinned
salt and freshly ground pepper

For the sauce
1 egg
50 g (2 oz) butter
15 ml (1 tbsp) boiling water
30 ml (2 level tbsp) made mustard
chopped fresh parsley to garnish

Put the artichokes in a saucepan with 15 ml (1 tbsp) lemon juice. Cover with cold water and bring to the boil, then reduce the heat and cook for 15–20 minutes until just tender when pierced with a knife. Drain, peel and thinly slice. Slice the tomatoes and arrange layers of artichokes and tomatoes in an ovenproof dish. Season well. Cover and keep warm.

For the sauce, blend together the egg, remaining lemon juice and seasoning. Melt the butter in a pan and gradually pour the melted butter onto the egg mixture, blending well all the time until thickened. Add the water and mustard and blend together for a few minutes. To serve warm, pour into a saucepan and heat very gently without boiling for 5 minutes. Pour over the artichokes and tomatoes and sprinkle with parsley.
Serves 4

Not suitable for freezing

Quick apricot jam

3 425-g (15-oz) cans apricot halves
30 ml (2 tbsp) lemon juice
450 g (1 lb) sugar

Drain the cans of apricots, reserving the syrup. Blend the apricots, a little at a time, with 300 ml ($\frac{1}{2}$ pint) of the syrup and the lemon juice and sugar, until smooth. Place in a saucepan and boil gently until thick. Pot and cover in the usual way.
Makes about 1.4 kg (3 lb).

Store in a cool, dry place

Apple chutney

1.4 kg (3 lb) onions, skinned
1.4 kg (3 lb) cooking apples, peeled and cored
thinly pared rind and juice of 2 lemons
450 g (1 lb) demerara sugar
600 ml (1 pint) malt vinegar
450 g (1 lb) sultanas

Roughly chop the onions and apples and put in a large saucepan with the lemon rind and juice, sugar and vinegar. Bring to the boil and simmer until really soft. Blend the mixture, a little at a time, until smooth. Return the mixture to the saucepan with the sultanas and cook for a further 15 minutes, or until thick. Pot and cover in the usual way.
Makes about 2 kg (4.5 lb).

Store in a cool, dry place

Carrot and olive salad

450 g (1 lb) carrots, peeled
50 g (2 oz) black olives, halved and stoned
60 ml (4 tbsp) chopped fresh parsley

For the dressing
salt and freshly ground pepper
2.5 ml ($\frac{1}{2}$ level tsp) French mustard
15 ml (1 tbsp) lemon juice
$\frac{1}{2}$–1 garlic clove, skinned and crushed
30 ml (2 tbsp) wine vinegar
60 ml (4 tbsp) vegetable oil

Grate the carrots finely and in a large bowl mix together with the olives and parsley. For the dressing blend the salt, pepper, mustard, lemon juice, garlic and vinegar well together. Blend in the oil gradually.

Just before serving, pour the dressing over the carrot mixture and mix well.
Serves 4–6

Not suitable for freezing

Tomato and marrow chutney

1.8 kg (4 lb) tomatoes, skinned
450 g (1 lb) marrow, peeled and seeded
225 g (8 oz) onions, skinned
15 g ($\frac{1}{2}$ oz) salt
pinch of cayenne pepper
1.25 ml ($\frac{1}{4}$ level tsp) paprika
1.25 ml ($\frac{1}{4}$ level tsp) ground cinnamon
1.25 ml ($\frac{1}{4}$ level tsp) ground allspice
1.25 ml ($\frac{1}{4}$ level tsp) ground cloves
1.25 ml ($\frac{1}{4}$ level tsp) ground ginger
5 ml (1 level tsp) mustard seeds
350 g (12 oz) sugar
300 ml ($\frac{1}{2}$ pint) malt vinegar

Finely chop the tomatoes, marrow and onions. Place all the ingredients except the sugar and vinegar in a large saucepan and simmer gently for 1$\frac{1}{2}$ hours until a thick pulp. Put the sugar and vinegar in a separate pan and heat gently until the sugar has dissolved. Add to the vegetable pulp and simmer gently for about 20 minutes until the chutney is thick and dark. Pot and cover in the usual way while hot.
Makes about 2.7 kg (6 lb).

Store in a cool, dry place

Red cabbage and beetroot salad

275 g (10 oz) red cabbage
225 g (8 oz) cooked beetroot, peeled
50 g (2 oz) onion, skinned
30 ml (2 tbsp) vegetable oil
15–30 ml (1–2 tbsp) red wine vinegar
salt and freshly ground pepper

Shred the cabbage, chop the beetroot and finely chop the onion. Combine in a salad bowl. Blend together the oil, vinegar and seasoning. Add the dressing to the salad and toss lightly until the cabbage is well coated. Leave for 30 minutes before serving.
Serves 6

Not suitable for freezing

Broccoli with orange butter sauce

450 g (1 lb) broccoli, trimmed
3 egg yolks
grated rind and juice of 1 orange
15 ml (1 tbsp) lemon juice
salt and freshly ground pepper
100 g (4 oz) unsalted butter, softened
30–45 ml (2–3 tbsp) double cream

Cook the broccoli in boiling salted water for 10–15 minutes until tender but still crisp. Drain well and keep warm.

Meanwhile make the sauce. Blend together the egg yolks, orange rind and juice, lemon juice and seasoning. Add the butter to the egg mixture beating well all the time until thickened. Stir in the cream. Pour into a saucepan and heat very gently, without boiling, for 5 minutes.

Place the broccoli on a warmed serving dish and serve immediately with the orange butter sauce.
Serves 4

Not suitable for freezing

Potatoes with fennel and soured cream

This potato dish is particularly good served with bacon chops.

700 g (1½ lb) potatoes, peeled
225 g (8 oz) head of fennel, trimmed
75 g (3 oz) butter or margarine
salt and freshly ground pepper
150 ml (¼ pint) soured cream

Thinly slice the potatoes and fennel. Layer a third of the potatoes in a shallow ovenproof dish. Cover with half the fennel, dot with half the fat and season liberally with salt and pepper. Spread with the soured cream. Cover with another layer of potato and the rest of the fennel. Finish with a final layer of sliced potato and dot with the remaining fat. Season again.

Cover and cook in the oven at 190°C (375°F)

mark 5 for about 45 minutes. Uncover and return to the oven for a further 35 minutes, until golden brown.
Serves 4

Not suitable for freezing

Rosemary jelly

Illustrated in colour facing page 80

Both the ripeness of the fruit and the time allowed for dripping affect the quantity of juice and therefore the quantity of jelly obtained. It makes a delicious alternative to mint jelly to serve with roast lamb.

2.3 kg (5 lb) cooking apples
1.1 litre (2 pints) water
30 ml (2 level tbsp) fresh rosemary leaves
1.1 litre (2 pints) vinegar
granulated or preserving sugar
green food colouring
sprigs of rosemary

Wash and roughly chop the apples. Put in a large saucepan with the water and rosemary. Bring to the boil, then simmer for about 45 minutes until soft and pulpy. Stir from time to time to prevent sticking. Add the vinegar and boil for 5 minutes.

Strain through a jelly bag or cloth and allow the juice to drain for at least 12 hours. Do not squeeze the bag or the jelly will be cloudy. Discard the pulp.

Measure the extract and return to the pan with 450 g (1 lb) sugar to every 600 ml (1 pint) extract. Stir until the sugar has dissolved, then boil rapidly, without stirring, for about 10 minutes until setting point is reached. Skim the surface with a metal spoon. Add a few drops of colouring and stir well. Pot and cover in the usual way, adding a sprig of rosemary to each jar before covering.

Store in a cool, dry place

Lettuce, orange and red pepper salad

1 Cos lettuce, washed
1 bunch of watercress, washed
1 small onion, skinned
3 large oranges, peeled
1 small red pepper, seeded
30 ml (2 tbsp) chopped fresh parsley

For the dressing
60 ml (4 tbsp) vegetable oil
grated rind and juice of 1 orange
1.25 ml ($\frac{1}{4}$ level tsp) dry mustard
salt and freshly ground pepper
1.25 ml ($\frac{1}{4}$ level tsp) sugar

Shred the lettuce, chop the watercress and finely chop the onion. Slice the oranges and thinly slice the red pepper. Blend together all the dressing ingredients and pour half the dressing over the lettuce, watercress, onion and parsley. Toss lightly. Arrange the orange slices in a pattern on top of the lettuce. Arrange the pepper slices in a pattern on top of the lettuce. Arrange the pepper slices over the orange and spoon over the remaining dressing.
Serves 4

Not suitable for freezing

Courgettes with walnut sauce

700 g (1$\frac{1}{2}$ lb) courgettes, washed and trimmed
salt and freshly ground pepper
75 g (3 oz) butter
40 g (1$\frac{1}{2}$ oz) flour
450 ml ($\frac{3}{4}$ pint) milk
145-g (5-oz) packet cream cheese with garlic and herbs
25 g (1 oz) walnuts

Slice the courgettes and cook in boiling salted water for 5 minutes and drain well. Melt 40 g (1$\frac{1}{2}$ oz) of the butter in a pan and sauté the courgettes for 10 minutes until tender but still crisp.

Meanwhile, blend the remaining butter, flour and milk together until smooth. Pour into a saucepan and bring to the boil, stirring all the time. Cook gently for 2 minutes until thickened. Remove the sauce from the heat and gradually beat in the cheese. Chop the walnuts and stir into the sauce with the seasoning. Return to the heat for 2–3 minutes but do not boil. Spoon the courgettes into a warm serving dish and pour over the sauce.
Serves 4

To freeze Freeze the sauce only in a rigid container. To serve, reheat the frozen sauce gently in a saucepan and serve as above with the courgettes.

Puddings
and
Desserts

Chocolate cream pots

50 g (2 oz) ratafia biscuits
15–30 ml (1–2 tbsp) brandy
15 ml (1 level tbsp) instant coffee powder
225 g (8 oz) plain cooking chocolate
3 eggs, separated
150 ml ($\frac{1}{4}$ pint) double cream

Divide the ratafias equally between six 150-ml ($\frac{1}{4}$-pint) soufflé dishes and spoon over the brandy. Add 150 ml ($\frac{1}{4}$ pint) boiling water to the coffee and stir until it is dissolved. Grate the chocolate and blend 175 g (6 oz) into the coffee until smooth. Reserve 50 g (2 oz) to decorate. Gradually blend in the egg yolks. Whisk the egg whites stiffly and fold into the chocolate mixture. Spoon the mixture into the dishes and place in a refrigerator to set. Whip the cream until stiff. Decorate with piped cream and the reserved grated chocolate.
Serves 6

To freeze Wrap the dishes with foil. To serve, thaw at room temperature for 3 hours.

Glazed pineapple choux buns

For the choux pastry
50 g (2 oz) butter
150 ml ($\frac{1}{4}$ pint) water
65 g (2$\frac{1}{2}$ oz) flour
2 eggs, beaten

For the filling
1 ripe pineapple
150 ml ($\frac{1}{4}$ pint) double cream
25 g (1 oz) ground almonds
10–15 ml (2–3 tsp) Cointreau

For the glaze
100 g (4 oz) butter
100 g (4 oz) brown sugar
60 ml (4 level tbsp) golden syrup
15 ml (1 tbsp) lemon juice
25 g (1 oz) blanched almonds, toasted
   and chopped

For the pastry, melt the butter in the water and bring to the boil. Remove from the heat and add the flour all at once. Beat until the paste is smooth and forms a ball in the centre of the pan. Allow to cool slightly, then beat in the eggs gradually, adding just enough to give a smooth, glossy mixture. Place the choux pastry in spoonfuls on to dampened baking sheets to make eight buns, leaving a space between each. Bake in the oven at 220°C (425°F) mark 7 for 25–30 minutes until well risen and crisp. Place on a wire rack, split in half and leave to cool.

For the filling, remove the skin from the pineapple. Cut the flesh from the hard central core and chop finely. Whip the cream until stiff and mix thoroughly with the pineapple, ground almonds and Cointreau. Fill the buns with the pineapple cream and pile on a dish.

For the glaze, warm the butter, sugar and syrup in a saucepan and stir until well blended. Boil for 1 minute, then stir in the lemon juice and nuts. Pour over the choux buns and serve immediately.
Makes 8

To freeze Freeze the choux buns only. Pack, unfilled, into a polythene bag. To serve, thaw wrapped at room temperature for 1$\frac{1}{2}$ hours. Place on a baking tray and reheat in the oven at 180°C (350°F) mark 4 for 5 minutes. Cool and fill as above.

Sugared apricot cakes

These apricot filled doughnuts are equally good at tea time or as dessert.

350 g (12 oz) flour
10 ml (2 level tsp) baking powder
75 g (3 oz) caster sugar
40 g (1½ oz) butter
2 eggs, beaten
15–30 ml (1–2 tbsp) milk
450 g (1 lb) apricots, slit open and stoned
vegetable oil for deep frying
caster sugar to coat

Sift together the flour and baking powder and stir in the sugar. Mix in the butter until the mixture resembles fine breadcrumbs. Add the eggs and milk and mix to a soft dough.

Divide the dough between the number of apricots used. Cover each whole apricot with a piece of dough and shape into a ball, making sure the apricot is completely enclosed. Seal well.

Heat the oil to 182°C (360°F), or until a small cube of bread takes 1 minute to brown. Cook three or four cakes at a time for 5 minutes, turning occasionally until golden brown on all sides. Remove from the pan, drain on kitchen paper towel and sprinkle with caster sugar. Serve hot or cold, with apricot sauce (see below).
Makes about 12

To freeze Leave to cool then wrap. To serve, thaw at room temperature for 3–4 hours.

Apricot sauce

450 g (1 lb) apricots, halved and stoned
50 g (2 oz) caster sugar
10 ml (2 tsp) brandy

Place the apricots in a pan with 45 ml (3 tbsp) water, cover and simmer gently for 10–15 minutes until tender. Blend the apricots to form a purée and return to the pan with the sugar and brandy. Heat gently for 2–3 minutes.

Serve with the sugared apricot cakes or with ice cream.
Serves 6

To freeze Cool and pour into a rigid container. To serve, thaw at room temperature for 4 hours and heat gently in a saucepan.

Blackberry and apple crumble layer

225 g (8 oz) blackberries, washed and hulled
350 g (12 oz) cooking apples, peeled and cored
15 ml (1 tbsp) lemon juice
125 g (5 oz) caster sugar
175 g (6 oz) butter
175 g (6 oz) flour
100 g (4 oz) semolina
5 ml (1 level tsp) cinnamon
150 ml (¼ pint) double cream

Place half the blackberries in a saucepan. Slice the apple and add to the pan with the lemon juice and 25 g (1 oz) sugar. Cover and simmer gently for 10 minutes.

Mix the fat into the flour until it resembles fine breadcrumbs. Add the remaining sugar, semolina and cinnamon.

Press half the crumble mixture into a loose-bottomed 20.5-cm (8-in) round cake tin. Cover with the cooked fruit and sprinkle over the remaining crumble mixture. Bake at 200°C (400°F) mark 6 for 30 minutes. Serve hot or cold decorated with whipped cream and the reserved blackberries.
Serves 6

To freeze Cool, open freeze before decorating and then wrap. To serve cold, unwrap and thaw at room temperature for 4 hours. To serve hot, cover with foil and reheat at 200°C (400°F) mark 6 for 35 minutes. Decorate as above.

Chilled plum brulée

450 g (1 lb) plums, halved and stoned
150 ml ($\frac{1}{4}$ pint) sweet red wine
175 g (6 oz) caster sugar
300 ml ($\frac{1}{2}$ pint) natural yogurt
50 g (2 oz) soft brown sugar

Place the plums in a saucepan with the wine and caster sugar and cook for 30 minutes until pulpy. Blend to form a purée and leave to cool. Stir in the yogurt and spoon into six individual flameproof dishes. Place in the frozen food compartment of a refrigerator or a freezer and leave for 2 hours.

Sprinkle the tops of the plum mixture with soft brown sugar and place under a hot grill for 3 minutes until the sugar caramelises. Serve immediately.
Serves 6

To freeze Leave the plum mixture, covered, in the frozen food compartment until required. To serve, place in the refrigerator for 2 hours, then sprinkle with sugar and finish as above.

Cranberry puffs

450 g (1 lb) fresh or frozen cranberries
225 g (8 oz) cream cheese
75 ml (5 tbsp) clear honey
75 g (3 oz) ground almonds
396-g (14-oz) packet puff pastry, thawed
icing sugar to decorate

Cook the cranberries with 30 ml (2 tbsp) water for about 30 minutes until soft and pulpy. Blend to form a purée and leave to cool.

Beat the cream cheese until smooth and add the honey and ground almonds. Fold in the cranberry purée.

Divide the pastry in half and roll into two 30.5-cm (12-in) squares. Cut each square into four 15-cm (6-in) squares. Divide the cranberry filling between the squares. Dampen the edges of the pastry and fold over to form triangles. Press the edges well together to seal, then scallop the edges. Place on a greased baking sheet and cook in the oven at 220°C (425°F) mark 7 for 30 minutes until well risen and golden brown. Dust with icing sugar and serve while still warm.
Makes 8

To freeze Cool and wrap, omitting the icing sugar. To serve, place on a baking sheet and reheat in the oven at 190°C (375°F) mark 5 for 20 minutes, dusting with icing sugar as above.

Damson fool

450 g (1 lb) damsons, washed
100 g (4 oz) caster sugar
30 ml (2 tbsp) sherry
150 ml ($\frac{1}{4}$ pint) double cream
150 ml ($\frac{1}{4}$ pint) cold custard
chopped walnuts to decorate

Place the damsons in a saucepan with the sugar and 150 ml ($\frac{1}{4}$ pint) water and stir over a gentle heat to dissolve the sugar. Cover and

Rosemary jelly (page 74)

simmer gently for about 30 minutes until the damsons are very soft and pulpy. Remove the stones and blend the fruit to form a purée. Leave until cold.

Stir the sherry into the fruit purée. Whip the cream until stiff and fold in the custard and cream. Divide between six or eight stemmed glasses. Chill for 1 hour, then decorate with the chopped nuts.
Serves 6–8

To freeze Spoon into individual dishes and cover, omitting the decoration. To serve, thaw in the refrigerator, covered, for 2 hours and decorate.

Glazed lemon and almond tart

3 large thin-skinned lemons
175 g (6 oz) granulated sugar
175 g (6 oz) shortcrust pastry
  (see page 57)
50 g (2 oz) butter
50 g (2 oz) caster sugar
1 egg, beaten
50 g (2 oz) ground almonds
75 g (3 oz) self raising flour
10 ml (2 level tsp) arrowroot

Thinly slice $1\frac{1}{2}$ lemons and place in a shallow frying pan with 300 ml ($\frac{1}{2}$ pint) water and the granulated sugar. Cover and simmer gently for 1 hour until the peel is tender. Carefully remove the lemon slices and leave to drain. Reserve the syrup. Squeeze the juice from the remaining lemons.

Roll out the pastry and use to line a 20.5-cm (8-in) fluted flan dish. Cream together butter and caster sugar until light and fluffy. Beat in the egg and lemon juice a little at a time. Fold in the ground almonds and flour. Spread the mixture over the bottom of the flan case. Bake in the oven at 180°C (350°F) mark 4 for 40–45 minutes until the filling is firm and golden. Cool on a wire rack.

Arrange the lemon slices around the outside edge of the tart. Bring the reserved syrup to the boil. Blend the arrowroot with a little water, add to the syrup and simmer gently, stirring until thickened. Pour the glaze over the tart and leave to cool.
Serves 6–8

To freeze Cool, open freeze and wrap. To serve, leave at room temperature for 3 hours.

Normandy apple flan

Illustrated in colour opposite

175 g (6 oz) shortcrust pastry
  (see page 57)
4 ripe pears, peeled and cored
1 large cooking apple, peeled and cored
25 g (1 oz) soft brown sugar
1.25 ml ($\frac{1}{4}$ level tsp) ground cinnamon
25 g (1 oz) fine semolina
30 ml (2 tbsp) Calvados
2 small red-skinned eating apples, cored
15 ml (1 tbsp) lemon juice
30 ml (2 level tbsp) apricot jam, sieved

Roll out the pastry and use to line a 21.5-cm (8-in) flan ring. Bake blind in the oven at 190°C (375°F) mark 5 for 15 minutes. Meanwhile chop the pears and cooking apple and place in a saucepan with the sugar and cinnamon and 45 ml (3 tbsp) water. Cover and simmer gently for 15 minutes.

Stir the semolina and Calvados into the fruit mixture and spoon into the flan case. Slice the eating apples into thin wedges and arrange around the top of the flan and brush them with the lemon juice. Return the flan to the oven for a further 15 minutes. Melt the jam in a saucepan with 10 ml (2 tsp) water and brush the glaze over the tart when cooked. Serve hot or cold.
Serves 6

To freeze Cool, open freeze and wrap. To serve, unwrap and leave at room temperature for 3 hours. To reheat, cover loosely with foil and reheat in the oven at 200°C (400°F) mark 6 for 20 minutes.

Normandy apple flan (above)

Walnut tart

175 g (6 oz) shortcrust pastry
  (see page 57)
100 g (4 oz) shelled walnuts
3 eggs, beaten
150 ml ($\frac{1}{4}$ pint) golden syrup
50 g (2 oz) margarine, melted
grated rind and juice of 1 orange
75 g (3 oz) soft dark brown sugar

Roll out the pastry and use to line a 19-cm
($7\frac{1}{2}$-in) loose-bottomed flan tin. Chop the walnuts, beat together with all the remaining ingredients and pour into the flan. Bake in the
oven at 180°C (350°F) mark 4 for 50–60
minutes until golden brown and firm to touch.
Serve hot or cold with cream.
Serves 6

To freeze Cool and wrap. To serve, thaw
loosely wrapped at room temperature for 4
hours. To serve hot, cover with foil and reheat
in the oven at 190°C (375°F) mark 5 for 35
minutes.

Walnut tart

Brown bread ice cream

300 ml ($\frac{1}{2}$ pint) double cream
150 ml ($\frac{1}{4}$ pint) single cream
2.5 ml ($\frac{1}{2}$ tsp) vanilla essence
grated rind of 1 lemon
50 g (2 oz) icing sugar, sifted
100 g (4 oz) fresh brown breadcrumbs
50 g (2 oz) soft brown sugar

Whisk together the creams until stiff. Fold in
the vanilla essence, lemon rind and icing sugar.
Spoon the mixture into an ice tray or shallow
rigid container and freeze for 1 hour or until
the cream is starting to freeze round the edges.

Meanwhile spread the breadcrumbs out on a
lightly oiled baking sheet and sprinkle over the
brown sugar. Bake in the oven at 200°C
(400°F) mark 6 for 10–15 minutes, stirring
occasionally, until the sugar caramelises and
the crumbs are golden brown. Leave to cool
and break up into crumbs again with a fork.
Beat the ice cream until smooth and stir in the
breadcrumbs. Spoon back into the container
and freeze until firm.
Serves 6

To freeze Cover and leave in the freezer until
required. To serve, leave in a refrigerator for
about 10 minutes, until it has softened slightly.

Strawberry liqueur creams

225 g (8 oz) strawberries, washed and hulled
25 g (1 oz) caster sugar
30 ml (2 tbsp) Kirsch
300 ml ($\frac{1}{2}$ pint) whipping cream

Reserve four whole strawberries for decoration. Slice half the remaining strawberries and
place in the bottom of four individual glass
dishes. Sprinkle over the caster sugar and
Kirsch. Whip the cream until stiff. Blend the
remaining strawberries to form a purée and
fold into the cream. Pile the strawberry cream
into the glass dishes and decorate with the
reserved strawberries.
Serves 4

To freeze Make the creams in freezer-proof dishes and cover. To serve, thaw covered in a refrigerator for 4 hours, or at room temperature for 2 hours. Serve chilled.

Mocha cheesecake

175 g (6 oz) butter
450 g (1 lb) chocolate coated digestive
   biscuits
225 g (8 oz) cream cheese
100 g (4 oz) caster sugar
10 ml (2 level tsp) instant coffee
10 ml (2 tsp) boiling water
100 g (4 oz) plain chocolate, broken
   into pieces
2 eggs, separated
300 ml ($\frac{1}{2}$ pint) double cream
coffee beans to decorate

Melt the butter in a large saucepan. Crush the biscuits and stir into the butter. Press the mixture over the base and sides of a 23-cm (9-in) loose-bottomed round cake tin. Leave to chill for 30 minutes in the refrigerator.

Beat the cream cheese and half the sugar together until smooth. Dissolve the coffee in the water in a heatproof bowl and add the chocolate. Stand the bowl over a pan of hot water until the chocolate has melted. Remove from the heat and beat in the egg yolks.

Fold the chocolate mixture into the cheese, then whisk the egg whites stiffly and fold these in too. Whip the cream until stiff and, reserving a little for decoration, fold it into the chocolate and cheese mixture. Pour the mixture into the biscuit case and leave to set for 2–3 hours. To serve, remove the tin and decorate with the reserved cream and a few coffee beans.
Serves 6–8

To freeze Open freeze and wrap. To serve, unwrap and thaw overnight in the refrigerator or for 4–5 hours at room temperature.

Creamy topped peach cake

450 g (1 lb) ripe peaches
175 g (6 oz) soft tub margarine
175 g (6 oz) soft brown sugar
3 eggs, beaten
vanilla essence
175 g (6 oz) self raising flour
150 ml ($\frac{1}{4}$ pint) double cream

Grease and line the sides and bottom of a 20.5-cm (8-in) cake tin. Reserve one peach for decoration and skin, stone and chop the remaining peaches. Cream together the margarine and sugar until light and fluffy. Beat in the eggs a little at a time with a few drops of vanilla essence. Fold in the flour and the chopped peaches. Spoon the mixture into the cake tin and smooth over the top. Bake in the oven at 180°C (350°F) mark 4 for 1–1$\frac{1}{4}$ hours until risen and golden brown. Remove from the tin and cool on a wire rack.

Whip the cream until stiff and spread over the top of the cake. Skin, stone and slice the remaining peach and scatter the slices over the cake.
Serves 6

To freeze Open freeze, then wrap. To serve, thaw unwrapped in the refrigerator for 4 hours.

Use your hand mixer to whisk egg whites and whip cream for desserts

Chocolate banana rum pie

100 g (4 oz) butter
175 g (6 oz) digestive biscuits
50 g (2 oz) caster sugar
45 ml (3 level tbsp) cornflour
568-ml (1-pint) carton
 chocolate-flavoured milk
50 g (2 oz) plain chocolate
1 medium banana, peeled
30 ml (2 tbsp) rum
150 ml ($\frac{1}{4}$ pint) soured cream
flaked almonds, toasted, to decorate

Melt the butter in a large saucepan. Crush the biscuits and stir into the butter with the sugar. Mix well and press into a 21.5-cm (8$\frac{1}{2}$-in) flan ring. Blend the cornflour with a little milk. Pour the remaining milk into a saucepan and bring to the boil, then pour on to the cornflour. Return to the pan, bring to the boil, stirring until thickened and remove from the heat. Grate the chocolate, stir into the filling and leave to cool slightly.

Blend the banana to form a purée and stir into the chocolate filling with the rum. Pour into the flan case. Leave in a cool place to set. Spoon the soured cream over the top of the flan and sprinkle a few flaked almonds on top to decorate.
Serves 4–6

To freeze Open freeze before adding the soured cream and nuts, then wrap in foil. To serve, thaw at room temperature for 2 hours.

Apple cherry flan

175 g (6 oz) shortcrust pastry
 (see page 57)
60 ml (4 level tbsp) black cherry jam
50 g (2 oz) ground almonds
450 g (1 lb) cooking apples, peeled and cored
2.5 ml ($\frac{1}{2}$ tsp) almond essence
2 egg whites
75 g (3 oz) caster sugar

Roll out the pastry and use to line a 19-cm (7$\frac{1}{2}$-in) flan ring. Bake blind in the oven at 190°C (375°F) mark 5 for 20 minutes. Spread the jam over the base of the flan case and sprinkle over the ground almonds.

Slice the apple and place in a saucepan with 60 ml (4 tbsp) water and the almond essence. Cover and simmer gently for 10 minutes until soft. Use a draining spoon to transfer the apple slices into the base of the flan case. Whisk the egg whites until stiff, whisk in half the sugar, then fold in the remaining sugar. Spoon or pipe the meringue over the flan. Return to the oven at 200°C (400°F) mark 6 for 4 minutes until the top is golden brown and crisp.
Serves 4

Not suitable for freezing

Golden treacle tart

175 g (6 oz) shortcrust pastry
 (see page 57)
75 g (3 oz) fresh white breadcrumbs
60 ml (4 level tbsp) golden syrup
30 ml (2 level tbsp) treacle
grated rind and juice of 1 lemon

Roll out the pastry on a lightly floured surface and use to line an 18-cm (7-in) flan ring. Roll out the trimmings and cut into strips 0.5 cm ($\frac{1}{4}$ in) in width. Mix together the breadcrumbs, syrup, treacle and lemon rind and juice. Spread the filling over the base of the pastry case and decorate the top with the pastry strips to form a lattice. Bake the tart in the oven at 200°C (400°F) mark 6 for 10 minutes then reduce the temperature to 190°C (375°F) mark 5 and bake for a further 15–20 minutes until golden brown. Serve hot or cold.
Serves 4–6

To freeze Cool and wrap. To serve, unwrap and thaw for 3 hours at room temperature. Serve cold or reheat at 190°C (375°F) mark 5 for 10 minutes.

Apricot almond pudding

**225 g (8 oz) fresh ripe apricots, washed
  and stoned**
450 ml (¾ pint) milk
25 g (1 oz) butter
100 g (4 oz) fresh white breadcrumbs
25 g (1 oz) ground almonds
2.5 ml (½ tsp) almond essence
75 g (3 oz) caster sugar
2 eggs, separated
few flaked almonds

Finely chop the apricots and place in the base
of a 1.1-litre (2-pint) ovenproof dish. In a
saucepan, heat the milk and butter together
until the butter has melted. Mix the breadcrumbs, ground almonds, almond essence, 25 g
(1 oz) of the sugar and egg yolks together. Beat
this mixture into the milk and pour over the
chopped apricots. Cover lightly with greaseproof paper and bake in the oven at 180°C
(350°F) mark 4 for 30 minutes until set.

Whisk the egg whites until stiff, whisk in half of
the remaining sugar and fold in the rest. Spoon
the meringue over the pudding and sprinkle
over the almonds. Bake in the oven at 200°C
(400°F) mark 6 for 4 minutes until golden
brown and crisp.
Serves 4

Not suitable for freezing

Raspberry and redcurrant water ice

100 g (4 oz) caster sugar
225 g (8 oz) redcurrants, washed
225 g (8 oz) raspberries, washed
15 ml (1 tbsp) Cointreau
15 ml (1 tbsp) lemon juice
2 egg whites

Dissolve the sugar in a saucepan with 300 ml
(½ pint) water over a low heat and bring to
the boil. Add the redcurrants, raspberries,
Cointreau and lemon juice, cover and simmer

gently for 10 minutes until the fruit is soft. Cool
slightly.

Blend the fruit and syrup together to form a
purée and strain into ice trays or a shallow
rigid container. Discard the pips left in the
sieve. Freeze the water ice until mushy and
turn into a large bowl. Stiffly whisk the egg
whites and fold into the fruit mixture. Return
to the ice trays and freeze until firm. Allow the
ice to soften slightly in the refrigerator for 10
minutes before serving.
Serves 6

To freeze Cover and leave in the freezer until
required. To serve, place covered in the refrigerator for 10 minutes.

Blender lemon pudding

*This pudding, just right for cold winter days,
cooks to a light sponge top with a tangy lemon
sauce underneath. When using a small, less
powerful blender, grate the lemon rind into the
goblet.*

1 large juicy lemon
2 eggs, separated
100 g (4 oz) caster sugar
50 g (2 oz) butter, softened
50 g (2 oz) self raising flour
300 ml (½ pint) milk

With a sharp knife or vegetable peeler pare the
rind from the lemon, free of any white pith, and
chop very finely. Squeeze the juice from the
lemon. Blend the rind, egg yolks, sugar, butter,
flour, milk and 45 ml (3 tbsp) lemon juice until
smooth. Whisk the egg whites until stiff and
fold in the lemon mixture. Spoon into a lightly
buttered 1.1-litre (2-pint) pie dish. Place the
dish in a roasting tin half filled with water and
bake in the oven at 180°C (350°F) mark 4 for
40–50 minutes until golden brown and lightly
set. Serve hot or cold.
Serves 4

Not suitable for freezing

85

Banana ice cream

2 large ripe bananas
30 ml (2 tbsp) lemon juice
300 ml ($\frac{1}{2}$ pint) single cream
300 ml ($\frac{1}{2}$ pint) double cream
100 g (4 oz) icing sugar, sifted

Peel the bananas, blend to form a purée and immediately mix with the lemon juice. Whip together the single and double cream until stiff. Fold the cream and icing sugar into the banana purée. Pour into a rigid container and put in the frozen food compartment of a refrigerator or in a freezer. Leave for 1 hour, until the mixture just begins to set around the edges. Whisk the frozen mixture until smooth, then return to the container and freeze for 2–4 hours until firm.
Serves 6

To freeze Cover and leave in the freezer until required. To serve, allow to soften slightly in the refrigerator for about 30 minutes.

Peach cheesecake

175 g (6 oz) butter
350 g (12 oz) digestive biscuits
100 g (4 oz) caster sugar
350 g (12 oz) cream cheese
juice of $\frac{1}{2}$ a lemon
2 eggs, separated
411-g (14$\frac{1}{2}$-oz) can peach slices
15 g ($\frac{1}{2}$ oz) powdered gelatine
150 ml ($\frac{1}{4}$ pint) double cream

Melt the butter in a large saucepan. Crush the biscuits and add to the butter with 25 g (1 oz) of the sugar. Mix well and press the mixture into the base of a 20.5-cm (8-in) round loose-bottomed cake tin. Cream together the cheese, remaining sugar and lemon juice until smooth, then beat in the egg yolks.

Drain the peaches, reserving the syrup. Place 60 ml (4 tbsp) of the syrup in a small bowl and sprinkle over the gelatine. Stand the bowl over

a saucepan of hot water and heat gently until the gelatine is dissolved. Leave to cool. Reserve eight peach slices for decoration and blend the rest to form a purée. Blend in the cheese mixture. Stir in the gelatine mixture and leave until just beginning to set.

Whisk the egg whites until stiff and fold into the peach mixture. Whip the cream until stiff and fold in, reserving a little for decoration. Spoon the peach mixture into the biscuit base and chill until set. To serve, carefully remove the tin and decorate with the reserved peaches and cream.
Serves 8

To freeze Open freeze before decorating, then wrap. To serve, thaw at room temperature for 2–3 hours then decorate as above.

Strawberry nut shortbread

50 g (2 oz) almonds, toasted
150 g (5 oz) plain flour
100 g (4 oz) butter, softened
65 g (2$\frac{1}{2}$ oz) caster sugar
150 ml ($\frac{1}{4}$ pint) whipping cream
225 g (8 oz) strawberries, washed and hulled

Strawberry nut shortbread

Roughly chop the almonds. Mix together the nuts, flour, butter and 50 g (2 oz) sugar to form a soft dough. Divide the mixture into four and press into 10-cm (4 in) rounds, or cut out the rounds with a fluted cutter. Place on a baking tray and bake in the oven at 170°C (325°F) mark 3 for 30 minutes until golden brown. Cool on a wire rack.

Lightly whip the cream and spread over the shortbread rounds. Arrange the strawberries on the top and sprinkle over the remaining sugar. Serve immediately.
Serves 4

Not suitable for freezing

Crumbed gooseberries

450 g (1 lb) gooseberries, topped and tailed
60 ml (4 level tbsp) golden syrup
50 g (2 oz) butter
100 g (4 oz) fresh white breadcrumbs
1.25 ml ($\frac{1}{4}$ level tsp) ground cinnamon
50 g (2 oz) demerara sugar
150 ml ($\frac{1}{4}$ pint) double cream

Place the gooseberries in a saucepan with 60 ml (4 tbsp) water, cover and simmer for 10–15 minutes until soft. Blend the gooseberries with the syrup to form a purée, then leave until cold. Melt the butter in a large frying pan and fry the breadcrumbs gently until they begin to colour. Mix the cinnamon and sugar and stir into the crumbs. Leave to cool.

Arrange alternate layers of gooseberry purée and the breadcrumb mixture in a glass dish, finishing with a layer of breadcrumbs. Whip the cream until stiff and spoon or pipe on top of the pudding.
Serves 4

To freeze Make the pudding in a freezer-proof dish and cover. To serve, thaw in the refrigerator for about 4 hours.

Venetian creams

Illustrated in colour on the jacket

350 g (12 oz) black grapes
1 egg white
100 g (4 oz) caster sugar
150 ml ($\frac{1}{4}$ pint) double cream
150 ml ($\frac{1}{4}$ pint) single cream
30–45 ml (2–3 tbsp) Amaretto or brandy

Reserve eight grapes for decoration and dip these in egg white and sprinkle with half the caster sugar. Leave to dry. Skin, halve and seed the remaining grapes. Whip together the creams until thick, then fold in the remaining sugar, Amaretto or brandy and grapes. Spoon into four individual glass dishes and chill for 1 hour. Decorate with the frosted grapes.
Serves 4

Not suitable for freezing

Home Baking

Luscious cider cake

175 g (6 oz) butter
175 g (6 oz) soft brown sugar
3 eggs
175 g (6 oz) self raising flour
45–60 ml (3–4 tbsp) sweet cider
300 ml ($\frac{1}{2}$ pint) double cream
15 ml (1 level tbsp) clear honey
25 g (1 oz) icing sugar, sifted
15 g ($\frac{1}{2}$ oz) walnuts

Grease two 19-cm ($7\frac{1}{2}$-in) sandwich tins. Cream together the butter and sugar, until light and fluffy. Gradually beat in the eggs one at a time. Mix in the flour and half the cider to form a soft dropping consistency and divide the mixture between the sandwich tins and smooth the top. Bake in the oven at 190°C (375°F) mark 5 for 35 minutes. Cool on a wire rack.

Whip the cream until thick and fold in the remaining cider, honey and icing sugar. Spread half the cream filling over one half of the sponge and sandwich together. Spread the remaining cream over the top, roughly chop the nuts and sprinkle over the cake.
Serves 8–10

To freeze Wrap the sponge cakes in foil before filling and decorating or pack into a rigid container. To serve, unwrap, thaw at room temperature for 2–3 hours then fill and decorate.

Cherry almond tarts

225 g (8 oz) flour
100 g (4 oz) ground almonds
175 g (6 oz) caster sugar
175 g (6 oz) butter
450 g (1 lb) red cherries, stoned
20 ml (4 level tsp) cornflour
60 ml (4 tbsp) brandy
50 g (2 oz) almonds
sifted icing sugar to decorate

For the pastry, mix together the flour, ground almonds and 50 g (2 oz) caster sugar. Mix in the butter and gradually work together into a ball. Take two-thirds of the pastry and press into four 10-cm (4-in) loose-bottomed fluted flan tins. Roll out the remaining pastry and cut into thin strips.

For the filling, cook the cherries with 300 ml ($\frac{1}{2}$ pint) water and the remaining sugar for 10 minutes until tender. Drain well, reserving the juices. Blend the cornflour with the brandy to a smooth paste, stir into the fruit juices and bring to the boil, stirring. Chop the almonds and add to the cornflour mixture with the cherries. Cool, then spoon into the pastry cases. Cover the tops with a close lattice of pastry strips. Bake in the oven at 200°C (400°F) mark 6 for 20–25 minutes. Leave to cool, then remove from the tins. Sprinkle with icing sugar before serving.
Serves 4

To freeze Open freeze then wrap. To serve, unwrap and thaw at room temperature for 3 hours.

Apple flapjack

900 g (2 lb) cooking apples, peeled and cored
65 g ($2\frac{1}{2}$ oz) sugar
150 g (5 oz) margarine
60 ml (4 level tbsp) golden syrup
225 g (8 oz) rolled oats
pinch of salt
5 ml (1 level tsp) ground ginger
sifted icing sugar to decorate

Slice the apples and simmer them gently in a covered saucepan with 40 g (1½ oz) sugar but no liquid for about 15 minutes until pulpy. Cool slightly, then blend to form a purée.

Line the bottom of an 18-cm (7-in) round loose-bottomed cake tin and brush with oil. Heat the remaining sugar with the margarine and syrup until dissolved. Stir in the oats, salt and ginger and mix well. Before it cools, line the bottom of the cake tin, and the sides up to 2.5 cm (1 in) from the rim, with three-quarters of the flapjack mixture.

Pour the apple purée into the centre and cover with the remaining flapjack mixture, pressing it down lightly. Bake in the oven at 190°C (375°F) mark 5 for 35 minutes. Cool for about 10 minutes before loosening the edges and removing from the tin. Serve warm or well chilled, dredged with icing sugar.
Serves 6

To freeze When cold, wrap in foil or pack into a polythene bag. To serve, thaw at room temperature for 4 hours.

Hazelnut yeast cake

15 g (½ oz) fresh yeast
175 ml (6 fl oz) tepid milk
450 g (1 lb) flour
2.5 ml (½ level tsp) salt
200 g (7 oz) butter
175 g (6 oz) hazel nuts, toasted
50 g (2 oz) digestive biscuits
175 g (6 oz) caster sugar
1 egg, beaten
25 g (1 oz) icing sugar, sifted

Grease a 900-g (2-lb) loaf tin. In a small bowl blend together the yeast and milk. Sift together the flour and salt and mix in 175 g (6 oz) butter until it resembles fine breadcrumbs. Add the yeast liquid and mix to form a soft dough. Knead for 5 minutes. Place in a bowl, cover with oiled polythene and leave in a warm place to rise for about 1 hour.

Chop the nuts and finely crush the biscuits and mix together with the sugar. Melt the remaining butter and use to bind the biscuit mixture together with the egg.

Knead the dough for 2–3 minutes and roll out to a 51 × 18-cm (20 × 7-in) oblong. Spread the filling over the dough and roll the two short ends in towards the centre. Place in the tin, seam down, cover again and leave in a warm place to prove for 30 minutes. Bake in the oven at 150°C (300°F) mark 2 for 1¼ hours. Cool on a wire rack. Mix the icing sugar with a little water and drizzle over the cake.
Serves 6

To freeze Open freeze the cooled cake, then wrap in foil or place in a polythene bag. To serve, unwrap and thaw at room temperature for 4 hours.

Yogurt drop scones

Orange rind is a good alternative to lemon rind.

150 ml (¼ pint) natural yogurt
1 egg
50 g (2 oz) plain flour
pinch of salt
grated rind of 1 lemon
30 ml (2 tbsp) lemon juice
vegetable oil for frying
caster sugar

Blend together the yogurt, egg, flour, salt and lemon rind and juice until smooth. Heat a little oil in a large frying pan. Add the mixture to the pan in 15 ml (1 tbsp) amounts and cook for 1–2 minutes on each side until golden brown. Remove from the pan and drain on kitchen paper towel. Keep warm while cooking the remaining mixture. Serve warm, sprinkled with caster sugar or spread with lemon curd.
Makes about 14

To freeze Cool and pack in a rigid container or polythene bag. To serve, unwrap and thaw at room temperature for 1 hour.

Sour cream loaf cake

100 g (4 oz) butter
225 g (8 oz) caster sugar
3 eggs
2.5 ml ($\frac{1}{2}$ tsp) vanilla essence
150 ml ($\frac{1}{4}$ pint) soured cream
225 g (8 oz) self raising flour
5 ml (1 level tsp) ground ginger
10 ml (2 level tsp) cinnamon
100 g (4 oz) mixed dried fruit
100 g (4 oz) icing sugar

Lightly grease and base-line a 900 g (2 lb) loaf tin. Cream together the butter and caster sugar until light and fluffy. Gradually beat in the eggs, vanilla essence and soured cream. Mix in the flour, spices and fruit. Pour the mixture into the prepared tin and bake in the oven at 180°C (350°F) mark 4 for 1 hour 40 minutes. Leave in the tin for 15 minutes then cool on a wire rack.

Sift the icing sugar and add a little warm water, beating well. The icing should be thick enough to coat the back of a spoon. Pour the icing over the top of the cake so a little runs down the sides.
Serves 10–12

To freeze Open freeze, then wrap in foil or place in a polythene bag. To serve, unwrap and thaw at room temperature for 4 hours.

Spicy fruit scones

225 g (8 oz) self raising flour
pinch of salt
50 g (2 oz) butter
25 g (1 oz) caster sugar
2.5 ml ($\frac{1}{2}$ level tsp) mixed spice
50 g (2 oz) currants
150 ml ($\frac{1}{4}$ pint) milk

Sift the flour and salt together. Mix the butter into the flour until it resembles fine bread-crumbs. Stir in the sugar, spice and currants. Add the milk, all at once, to form a soft dough.

Roll out on a floured surface to 2-cm ($\frac{3}{4}$-in) thick. Cut into ten to twelve rounds with a 5-cm (2-in) cutter. Place on a baking sheet and bake in the oven at 230°C (450°F) mark 8 for 10 minutes until well risen and golden brown. Cool on a wire rack, but serve while still slightly warm, with butter.
Makes 10–12

To freeze When cold, pack into a polythene bag. To serve, thaw at room temperature for 3 hours or reheat from frozen in the oven at 180°C (350°F) mark 4 for 15–20 minutes.

Walnut cake

75 g (3 oz) shelled walnuts
150 g (5 oz) butter
225 g (8 oz) self raising flour
pinch of salt
150 g (5 oz) caster sugar
3 eggs, beaten
milk

Grease and line an 18-cm (7-in) cake tin. Reserve a few walnuts for decoration and roughly chop the rest. Mix the butter into the flour and salt until it resembles fine bread-crumbs. Mix in the sugar and the eggs. Add a little milk if necessary to form a soft dropping consistency and spoon the mixture into the cake tin. Arrange the reserved nuts on top.

Do not stand at my grave and weep;
I am not there. I do not sleep.
I am a thousand winds that blow,
I am the diamond glints on snow......

I am the sunlight on ripened grain,
I am the gentle autumn rain ....

When you awaken in the mornings hush,
I am the swift uplifting rush
of quiet birds in circled flight,
I am the soft stars that shine at night.
Do not stand at my grave and cry;
I am not there. I did not die.

anon

G082 Floral Tribute 2 by Jane Ormes

price
code GH45
Canada 3.95

© **PAPERLINK**
356 Kennington Road London SE11 4LD 020 7582 8244
Printed in England on paper from trees grown in sustainable forests

5 018930 080820

Bake in the oven at 180°C (350°F) mark 4 for $1\frac{1}{4}$–$1\frac{1}{2}$ hours. Cool on a wire rack.
Serves 6–8

To freeze Wrap in foil. To serve, thaw at room temperature for 4 hours.

Chocolate cinnamon slices

Illustrated in colour facing page 97

450 g (1 lb) plain cooking chocolate
225 g (8 oz) butter
30 ml (2 level tbsp) golden syrup
10 ml (2 level tsp) ground cinnamon
2 eggs
450 g (1 lb) digestive biscuits

Break the chocolate into pieces and place in a saucepan with the butter and syrup. Heat gently, stirring, until the chocolate has melted. Add the cinnamon and stir well together. Remove from the heat and beat in the eggs. Crush the biscuits, stir into the chocolate mixture and mix well. Spoon into a 900-g (2-lb) loaf tin, place in a refrigerator and leave overnight or until firm. To serve, turn out and cut into slices.
Makes 20 slices

To freeze Wrap in foil. To serve, thaw unwrapped at room temperature for 3 hours.

Chocolate cherry cake

Illustrated in colour facing page 97

100 g (4 oz) butter
100 g (4 oz) caster sugar
2 eggs
100 g (4 oz) self raising flour
50 g (2 oz) plain chocolate
50 g (2 oz) glacé cherries
30 ml (2 tbsp) milk
175 g (6 oz) icing sugar
glacé cherries, halved, to decorate

Lightly grease and flour a 16-cm ($6\frac{1}{2}$-in) round cake tin. Cream together the butter and sugar until light and fluffy. Beat in the eggs. Mix in the flour. Chop the chocolate and cherries finely and stir into the mixture with the milk. Spoon into the prepared tin and smooth the top. Bake in the oven at 170°C (325°F) mark 3 for 1 hour. Leave to cool for a few minutes then turn out on to a wire rack. Sift the icing sugar into a bowl and add 15–30 ml (1–2 tbsp) warm water until the icing is thick enough to coat the back of a spoon. Spread over the cake and decorate with the cherries.
Serves 6–8

To freeze Wrap in foil or a polythene bag. To serve, unwrap and thaw at room temperature for 4 hours.

Apricot bars

100 g (4 oz) dried apricots
75 g (3 oz) self raising flour
75 g (3 oz) rolled oats
75 g (3 oz) light brown soft sugar
100 g (4 oz) butter

Lightly grease a 28 × 18 × 4-cm (11 × 7 × $1\frac{1}{2}$-in) tin. Soak the apricots in water overnight then drain. Mix together the flour, oats and sugar. Add the butter and mix until it resembles fine breadcrumbs. Spread half the mixture over the base of the prepared tin.

Roughly chop the apricots and spread over the base. Sprinkle over the remaining crumb mixture and press down well. Bake in the oven at 190°C (375°F) mark 5 for 25 minutes until golden brown. Leave in the tin for 15 minutes, then turn out and cut into twelve bars.
Makes 12

To freeze When cold, wrap in foil or pack into a rigid container. To serve, unwrap and thaw at room temperature for 3 hours.

Date and hazelnut rings

15 g ($\frac{1}{2}$ oz) fresh yeast
225 ml (8 fl oz) tepid milk
450 g (1 lb) strong white flour
5 ml (1 level tsp) salt
50 g (2 oz) butter
1 egg, beaten
175 g (6 oz) dates
100 g (4 oz) glacé cherries
75 g (3 oz) hazel nuts
2.5 ml ($\frac{1}{2}$ level tsp) mixed spice
15 ml (1 level tbsp) dark brown soft sugar
milk
225 g (8 oz) icing sugar

Lightly grease a baking sheet. Blend together the yeast and milk. Sift 150 g (5 oz) flour and the salt into a large bowl. Add the yeast liquid and leave in a warm place for about 20 minutes until frothy. Mix the butter into the remaining flour until it resembles fine breadcrumbs. Add the egg and the yeast batter to the flour mixture and mix well to form a soft dough. Knead for 10 minutes until smooth and no longer sticky, then cover with lightly oiled polythene and leave to rise in a warm place for about 1 hour until doubled in size.

Meanwhile, make the filling. Roughly chop the dates, 75 g (3 oz) cherries and 50 g (2 oz) nuts. Mix together with the spice and sugar. Divide the dough into 6 pieces and roll out each piece to a 12.5 × 7.5-cm (5 × 3-in) oblong. Divide the filling equally between the pieces of dough. Brush the edges with milk, then roll up from the long edges and seal well. Form each roll into a ring, join the edges together and place on the prepared baking sheet. Cover with the lightly oiled polythene and leave to prove until doubled in size.

Bake the hazelnut rings in the oven at 200°C (400°F) mark 6 for 25 minutes until risen and golden brown. Cool on a wire rack. Roughly chop the remaining nuts and cherries for the topping. Sift the icing sugar and add 30–45 ml (2–3 tbsp) warm water, to make an icing thick enough to coat the back of a spoon. Coat the rings with the icing and decorate with the nuts and cherries.
Makes 6

To **freeze** Open freeze, then wrap in foil or pack into a rigid container. To serve, unwrap and thaw at room temperature for 3 hours.

Orange and sultana cake

75 g (3 oz) butter or margarine
198-g (7-oz) can condensed milk
2 eggs, beaten
175 g (6 oz) self raising flour
100 g (4 oz) sultanas
grated rind and juice of 1 small orange

Grease and line an 18-cm (7-in) cake tin. Cream the butter or margarine until soft and light. Gradually beat in the condensed milk, then the beaten eggs. Mix in the flour, sultanas and orange rind and juice, until well mixed. Turn the mixture into the cake tin and bake in the oven at 170°C (325°F) mark 3 for about 1 hour, until risen and golden brown. Cool on a wire rack.
Serves 8

To **freeze** Cool then wrap in foil or place in a polythene bag. To serve, unwrap and thaw at room temperature for 4 hours.

Walnut crunchies

Illustrated in colour facing page 97

90 g (3$\frac{1}{2}$ oz) butter
90 g (3$\frac{1}{2}$ oz) demerara sugar
1 egg
75 g (3 oz) shelled walnuts
175 g (6 oz) self raising flour
grated rind of 1 lemon
sifted icing sugar to decorate

Grease two baking sheets. Cream together the butter and sugar until light and fluffy. Beat in the egg. Chop the nuts and mix in with the flour and lemon rind to form a stiff dough. Shape into a long roll, wrap in foil and chill in

Battenberg cake

225 g (8 oz) butter
225 g (8 oz) caster sugar
4 eggs
225 g (8 oz) self raising flour
few drops of vanilla essence
15 g ($\frac{1}{2}$ oz) cocoa powder, sifted
raspberry jam, warmed
caster sugar

For the marzipan
50 g (2 oz) icing sugar, sifted
50 g (2 oz) caster sugar
100 g (4 oz) ground almonds
few drops of vanilla essence
$\frac{1}{2}$ a beaten egg
lemon juice

Wrap marzipan round the sponge strips to complete assembly of the Battenberg cake

Grease and line a Swiss roll tin. Divide lengthways with a greaseproof paper or foil 'wall'. Cream together the butter and sugar. Beat in the eggs and mix in the flour and vanilla essence. Spoon half the mixture into the tin. Add the cocoa to the remaining mixture and spoon into the other half of the tin. Bake in the oven at 190°C (375°F) mark 5 for 45–50 minutes until well risen. Remove from the tin and cool on a wire rack.

Meanwhile mix together the marzipan ingredients, adding enough lemon juice to form a stiff dough. Form into a ball and knead lightly.

Trim the brown and white cakes to equal sizes and cut each in half lengthways. Spread the sides of the strips with the jam and stick them together, alternating the colours and pressing the pieces well together. Coat the whole outside of the cake with jam. Roll out the marzipan thinly on a surface dusted with caster sugar to a 20.5 × 25.5-cm (8 × 10-in) oblong. Wrap around the cake, seal well and trim the edges. Crimp along the top outer edges to make a decorative border. Score the top with a sharp knife to give a criss-cross pattern.
Serves 8

To freeze Wrap in foil or place in a polythene bag. To serve, unwrap and thaw at room temperature for 4 hours.

Dark honey teabread

100 g (4 oz) plain flour
5 ml (1 level tsp) cinnamon
5 ml (1 level tsp) bicarbonate of soda
pinch of salt
45 ml (3 tbsp) vegetable oil
30 ml (2 tbsp) clear honey
30 ml (2 tbsp) golden syrup
50 g (2 oz) demerara sugar
1 egg
30 ml (2 tbsp) milk
75 g (3 oz) sultanas
butter

For the topping
15 g ($\frac{1}{2}$ oz) glacé cherries
15 g ($\frac{1}{2}$ oz) shelled walnuts
15 ml (1 tbsp) clear honey

Lightly grease and base-line a 450-g (1-lb) loaf tin. Mix together all the teabread ingredients. Pour into the prepared tin and bake in the oven at 180°C (350°F) mark 4 for 1 hour. Cool in the tin for a few minutes, then turn out and cool. Roughly chop the cherries and walnuts for the topping. Brush the top of the cake with the honey, then sprinkle over the cherries and nuts. Serve sliced and spread with butter.
Serves 8

To freeze Open freeze, then wrap in foil. To serve, unwrap and thaw at room temperature for 4 hours.

Tenderloin casserole (page 116), Sliced jacket potatoes and Parsnip and carrot au gratin (page 117)

Honey chip cookies

Illustrated in colour opposite

These cakelike cookies keep fresh in an airtight jar.

100 g (4 oz) butter
50 g (2 oz) caster sugar
175 g (6 oz) thick honey
1 egg
2.5 ml ($\frac{1}{2}$ tsp) vanilla essence
175 g (6 oz) self raising flour
pinch of salt
75 g (3 oz) almonds
75 g (3 oz) plain chocolate

Lightly grease two baking sheets. Cream together the butter, sugar and honey until light and fluffy. Beat in the egg and vanilla essence. Mix in the flour and salt. Chop the almonds and chocolate and add to the mixture. Place small spoonfuls on the baking sheets, allowing plenty of room to spread. Bake in the oven at 190°C (375°F) mark 5 for 15 minutes until golden brown. Allow to firm up slightly before transferring to a wire rack to cool.
Makes 32

To freeze Cool and pack into a rigid container. To serve, unpack and thaw at room temperature for $1\frac{1}{2}$–2 hours.

Quick white bread

15 g ($\frac{1}{2}$ oz) fresh yeast
300 ml ($\frac{1}{2}$ pint) tepid water
450 g (1 lb) strong white flour
5 ml (1 level tsp) salt

Lightly grease two 450 g (1-lb) loaf tins. Blend together the yeast and water. Sift together the flour and salt and add the yeast liquid. Mix well to form an elastic dough, adding a little more water if necessary. Knead for 10 minutes until really smooth.

Divide the dough into two portions and place in the tins. Cover the tins with lightly oiled polythene and leave to rise in a warm place for about 1 hour until the dough comes to the top of the tins and springs back when gently pressed with a floured finger. Bake in the oven at 230°C (450°F) mark 8 for 25 minutes. Turn out and cool on a wire rack.

To make rolls, divide the dough into eight pieces and proceed as above, allowing 15–20 minutes for baking.
Makes two 450 g (1 lb) loaves or 8 rolls

To freeze When cold, wrap in foil or pack into a polythene bag. To serve, thaw the bread wrapped at room temperature for 3–4 hours and rolls for 1–2 hours.

Almond fingers

225 g (8 oz) self raising flour
100 g (4 oz) butter
225 g (8 oz) marzipan (see page 96)
225 g (8 oz) caster sugar
2 eggs
2.5 ml ($\frac{1}{2}$ tsp) vanilla essence
sifted icing sugar to decorate

Mix together the flour and butter until it resembles fine breadcrumbs. Add 100 ml (4 fl oz) cold water and mix to form a soft dough. Cover and chill for 1 hour.

Beat together the marzipan, sugar, eggs and vanilla essence. On a lightly floured surface roll out half of the dough and use to line the base and sides of a shallow 26.5 × 18-cm ($10\frac{1}{2}$ × 7-in) baking dish. Spread the filling over the base. Roll out the remaining dough to cover the top and seal the edges. Bake in the oven at 200°C (400°F) mark 6 for 30–35 minutes. Cool and cut into sixteen fingers. Sprinkle with icing sugar.
Makes 16

To freeze Wrap in foil or pack into a rigid container. To serve, allow to thaw at room temperature for 4 hours.

Chocolate cinnamon slices and Chocolate cherry cake (page 93),
Walnut crunchies (page 94), Honey chip cookies (above),
Ginger orange squares (page 98)

Ginger orange squares

Illustrated in colour facing page 97

40 g (1½ oz) crystallised ginger
grated rind and juice of 1 medium orange
100 g (4 oz) butter
100 g (4 oz) self raising flour
2.5 ml (½ level tsp) baking powder
2.5 ml (½ level tsp) ground ginger
pinch of salt
50 g (2 oz) caster sugar
30 ml (2 tbsp) black treacle
2 eggs

For the icing
grated rind and juice of 1 medium orange
50 g (2 oz) butter
225 g (8 oz) icing sugar, sifted

Lightly grease and base-line an 18-cm (7-in) square cake tin. Chop the crystallised ginger finely and reserve 15 g (½ oz) for decoration. Mix together the remaining cake ingredients until smooth and pour into the tin. Bake in the oven at 180°C (350°F) mark 4 for 30 minutes until risen and firm. Leave in the tin for a few minutes, then turn out and cool on a wire rack.

Beat together the icing ingredients until smooth. Spread the butter icing over the cake and cut into sixteen squares. Place a piece of the reserved ginger on the top of each square.
Makes 16

To freeze Open freeze, then pack into a rigid container. To serve, thaw uncovered at room temperature for 3 hours.

Lemon butter loaf cake

100 g (4 oz) butter
100 g (4 oz) light brown soft sugar
100 g (4 oz) self raising flour
2 eggs
grated rind and juice of 1 lemon
sifted icing sugar to decorate

Lightly grease and base-line a 450-g (1-lb) loaf tin. Mix together the butter, brown sugar, flour, eggs and lemon rind and juice. Beat until smooth. Pour the mixture into the loaf tin and bake in the oven at 180°C (350°F) mark 4 for 1¼ hours. Leave in the tin for a few minutes, then cool on a wire rack. Sprinkle with sifted icing sugar and serve.
Serves 8

To freeze Wrap the cooled cake in foil. To serve, unwrap and thaw at room temperature for 4 hours.

Carrot cake

Illustrated in colour on the jacket

225 g (8 oz) carrots, peeled
100 g (4 oz) blanched almonds
225 g (8 oz) butter
225 g (8 oz) caster sugar
4 eggs
225 g (8 oz) self raising flour
grated rind and juice of 1 lemon
15 ml (1 tbsp) Kirsch
225 g (8 oz) icing sugar
75 g (3 oz) marzipan
orange food colouring
angelica

Grease and line a 20.5-cm (8-in) round cake tin. Grate the carrots. Chop the almonds finely. Cream the butter and caster sugar together until light and fluffy and beat in the eggs. Mix in the flour, lemon rind and juice (reserving 10 ml [2 tsp] juice), Kirsch, grated carrot and almonds.

Spoon the mixture into the cake tin. Bake in the oven at 180°C (350°F) mark 4 for 1½ hours until well risen and golden brown. After 1¼ hours cover with foil to prevent over browning. The cake is cooked when a skewer inserted in the centre comes out clean. Cool on a wire rack.

Preferably keep the cake until the following day before icing and serving. Sift the icing sugar into a bowl and add the reserved lemon juice and about 15 ml (1 tbsp) warm water. The icing should be thick enough to coat the back of a spoon. Spread the icing on top of the cake. Colour the marzipan with the orange food colouring and shape into small carrots; use the angelica for carrot tops. Decorate the cake with the carrots.
Serves 8

To freeze Wrap the cake in foil or a polythene bag before icing. To serve, unwrap and allow to thaw at room temperature for about 3 hours, then ice and decorate as above.

Apple potato cake

450 g (1 lb) old potatoes, peeled
25 g (1 oz) butter
100 g (4 oz) self raising flour
pinch of salt
2.5 ml (½ level tsp) cinnamon
1 egg
3 medium cooking apples
15 ml (1 tbsp) lemon juice
30 ml (2 level tbsp) demerara sugar

Lightly grease a baking sheet. Cook the potatoes in boiling salted water for 25 minutes until tender. Drain and blend with the butter until smooth. Beat in the flour, salt, cinnamon and egg and leave to cool slightly. Turn on to a lightly floured surface and knead lightly. Divide into two and roll out to form two 18-cm (7-in) rounds. Place on the baking sheet.

Peel, core and grate the apples. Add the lemon juice and 15 ml (1 level tbsp) sugar. Spoon over one half of the dough. Top with the remaining round of dough. Make a crimped edge and sprinkle with the remaining sugar.

Bake in the oven at 170°C (325°F) mark 3 for 40 minutes, until golden brown and serve.
Serves 6–8

To freeze When cold, wrap in foil or pack into a rigid container. To serve, unwrap and thaw at room temperature for 3 hours.

Chocolate blackcurrant gâteau

50 g (2 oz) plain chocolate
2 eggs
100 g (4 oz) soft margarine
100 g (4 oz) caster sugar
100 g (4 oz) self raising flour
225 g (8 oz) blackcurrants
50 g (2 oz) granulated sugar
15 ml (1 level tbsp) arrowroot
150 ml (¼ pint) whipping cream

Grease and base-line a 21.5-cm (8½-in) sandwich tin.

Melt the chocolate with 30 ml (2 tbsp) water in a bowl over a saucepan of hot water. Leave to cool. Blend the still liquid chocolate, the eggs, margarine, caster sugar and flour together for a few seconds. Pour the mixture into the prepared tin and bake in the oven at 190°C (375°F) mark 5 for about 30 minutes until risen and firm to the touch. Turn out and cool on a wire rack.

Meanwhile, place the blackcurrants, granulated sugar and 150 ml (¼ pint) water in a saucepan and cook until soft. Blend the arrowroot with a little water, stir into the currants then bring to the boil, stirring until clear.

Split the chocolate cake in half. Whip the cream until stiff. Fold the cold blackcurrant mixture into the cream and use to sandwich the cake. Eat the same day.
Serves 8–10

To freeze Pack the cake and blackcurrants separately, without the cream. To serve, allow to thaw at room temperature for about 5 hours, then finish as above.

Entertaining

Carrot and watercress soup	Sherried turkey suprêmes	Pashka
	Golden topped potato bake	
	Cabbage sauté	

Carrot and watercress soup

350 g (12 oz) carrots, peeled
1 large onion, skinned
1 bunch watercress, washed
45 ml (3 tbsp) vegetable oil
1.1 litre (2 pints) chicken stock
salt and freshly ground pepper

Roughly chop all of the vegetables, reserving a few sprigs of watercress for the garnish. Heat the oil in a large saucepan and gently fry the vegetables for 10 minutes. Add the stock and seasoning. Bring to the boil, cover and simmer for 20 minutes. Blend the soup to form a purée and reheat if necessary. Serve in a warm bowl garnished with the sprigs of watercress.
Serves 6

To freeze Cool quickly then pour into a rigid container, omitting the garnish. To serve, reheat the frozen soup gently and garnish as above.

Sherried turkey suprêmes

six 175 g (6 oz) turkey breasts, boned
1 small red pepper, seeded
225 g (8 oz) tomatoes
15 ml (1 tbsp) chopped fresh parsley
salt and freshly ground pepper
60 ml (4 tbsp) medium dry sherry
25 g (1 oz) butter
40 g (1½ oz) fresh white breadcrumbs
pinch of paprika

Split each turkey breast almost in half horizontally and beat out thinly. Place three of the breasts side by side in an ovenproof dish. Slice the pepper finely and blanch in boiling water for 2 minutes, then drain. Roughly chop the tomatoes. Layer the pepper, tomato, parsley and seasoning on top of the turkey. Cover with the remaining supremes.

Spoon over the sherry, cover and cook in the oven at 180°C (350°F) mark 4 for 30 minutes. Melt the butter in a frying pan and fry the breadcrumbs and paprika until golden brown. Sprinkle over the turkey before serving.
Serves 6

To freeze Cool quickly, then cover the dish or pack in a rigid container before adding the breadcrumbs. To serve, reheat the frozen turkey in the oven at 200°C (400°F) mark 6 for 1 hour and garnish with the breadcrumbs as above.

Golden topped potato bake

1.1 kg (2½ lb) large potatoes
salt and freshly ground pepper
568 ml (1 pint) milk
25 g (1 oz) butter

Peel the potatoes and slice. Layer with the seasoning in a shallow ovenproof dish. Pour over the milk and dot with butter. Bake in the oven at 180°C (350°F) mark 4 for 1¾ hours, until the potatoes are tender and the top golden.
Serves 6

Not suitable for freezing

Cabbage sauté

1 large cabbage
1 medium green pepper, seeded
1 large onion, skinned
75 g (3 oz) butter
salt and freshly ground pepper
grated nutmeg

Shred the cabbage finely. Slice the pepper and onion. Blanch the cabbage and pepper in boiling water for 2 minutes, then drain. Melt the butter in a saucepan and fry the onion for 5 minutes until soft. Add the cabbage, pepper, seasoning and nutmeg. Cover and cook for 5 minutes until just tender.
Serves 6

Not suitable for freezing

Pashka

This sweet dish was originally made in Russia and is traditionally served at Easter with cake.

15 g ($\frac{1}{2}$ oz) glacé cherries
450 g (1 lb) curd cheese
50 g (2 oz) caster sugar
1 egg yolk
1.25 ml ($\frac{1}{4}$ tsp) vanilla essence
15 g ($\frac{1}{2}$ oz) sultanas
15 g ($\frac{1}{2}$ oz) flaked almonds
150 ml ($\frac{1}{4}$ pint) whipping cream
25 g (1 oz) almond nibs

Roughly chop the cherries. Beat together all the ingredients except the almond nibs, reserving a little cream for decoration. Line a sieve with a clean 'J' cloth or piece of muslin. Spoon the cream cheese mixture into the sieve and leave to drain over a bowl for 4 hours in the refrigerator.

Turn the mixture on to a plate and remove the muslin. Toast the almond nibs under a hot grill until golden brown, then cool. Press the almond nibs over the pashka. Whip the reserved cream and pipe around the edge of the pashka to decorate.
Serves 6

To freeze Open freeze before decorating with the almonds and cream, then wrap in foil. To serve, thaw in the refrigerator overnight and decorate as above.

Pashka

Orange, date and walnut appetiser   Lamb maître d'hôtel   Baked Austrian cheesecake
Risotto
Creamy dill carrots

Orange, date and walnut appetiser

4 medium oranges
100 g (4 oz) Cheddar cheese
25 g (1 oz) shelled walnuts
8 silverskin onions, skinned
grated rind of $\frac{1}{2}$ a lemon
30 ml (2 level tbsp) mayonnaise
freshly ground pepper
100 g (4 oz) fresh dates, halved
   and stoned

For the dressing
15 ml (1 tbsp) orange juice
15 ml (1 tbsp) lemon juice
5 ml (1 tsp) white vinegar
30 ml (2 tbsp) corn oil

Finely grate the rind from half of one orange and pare the rind from the other half and cut into fine julienne strips. Peel all the oranges, removing all traces of white pith. Slice thinly, catching any juice from the oranges to use for the dressing.

Grate the cheese, chop the walnuts and onions and mix together thoroughly with the lemon and orange rind, mayonnaise and pepper. Arrange the orange slices on six individual plates. Divide the cheese mixture and spoon on to the centre of the oranges. Arrange halved dates round the cheese and top with strips of orange rind. Chill for 30 minutes.

Blend together the ingredients for the dressing and pour over the appetisers just before serving.
Serves 6

Not suitable for freezing

Lamb maître d'hôtel

six 2 cm ($\frac{3}{4}$ in) thick lean lamb chump chops
50 g (2 oz) butter
1 garlic clove, skinned and crushed
chopped fresh parsley
grated rind and juice of $\frac{1}{2}$ a lemon
salt and freshly ground pepper
watercress to garnish

Trim any excess fat from the chops. Using a sharp knife make a pocket in the side of the chops away from the bone. Beat the butter to soften, add the remaining ingredients and beat well. Press the butter well into the pockets and seal with wooden cocktail sticks.

Place the chops in a roasting tin, loosely covered with foil. Cook in the oven at 190°C (375°F) mark 5 for 45 minutes, turning the chops half way through cooking time. Serve garnished with watercress.
Serves 6

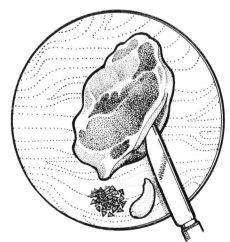

Cut a pocket in the side of each chop to contain the maître d'hôtel butter

To **freeze** Cool quickly then wrap in foil, omitting the garnish. To serve, place the frozen foil-wrapped chops on a baking tray and reheat at 190°C (375°F) mark 5 for 1 hour.

Risotto

225 g (8 oz) streaky bacon
1 large onion, skinned
4 large tomatoes, skinned
275 g (10 oz) long grain rice
900 ml (1½ pints) chicken stock
salt and freshly ground pepper
chopped fresh parsley to garnish

Remove the rind and roughly chop the bacon. Roughly chop the onion and tomatoes. Cook the bacon in a large frying pan until crisp and the fat begins to run. Remove from the pan and add the onion and rice and fry in the bacon fat until well coloured. Stir the tomatoes into the rice and cook for 2 minutes. Add the stock and seasoning and bring to the boil. Turn into an ovenproof dish. Cover and cook in the oven at 190°C (375°F) mark 5 for 40 minutes. Stir in the bacon pieces and cook for a further 10 minutes.
Serves 6

Not suitable for freezing

Creamy dill carrots

700 g (1½ lb) carrots, peeled
300 ml (½ pint) milk
300 ml (½ pint) chicken stock
75 g (3 oz) butter
salt and freshly ground pepper
25 g (1 oz) flour
150 ml (¼ pint) single cream
10 ml (2 tsp) chopped fresh dill

Slice the carrots and place in a saucepan with the milk, stock, 25 g (1 oz) butter and seasoning. Bring to the boil, cover and simmer for about 30 minutes until tender. Drain and reserve the cooking liquid.

Blend together the cooking liquid, remaining butter and flour. Pour into a saucepan, bring to the boil, whisking, and cook for 2 minutes until thickened. Stir in the carrots, cream and dill and reheat gently without boiling. Transfer to a heated serving dish.
Serves 6

To **freeze** Cool quickly then pack in a rigid container and cover. To serve, reheat from frozen, covered, in the oven at 180°C (350°F) mark 4 for 45–50 minutes.

Baked Austrian cheesecake

50 g (2 oz) digestive biscuits
450 g (1 lb) cottage cheese
150 ml (¼ pint) milk
50 g (2 oz) cornflour
2 eggs, separated
150 g (5 oz) caster sugar
5 ml (1 tsp) lemon juice
150 mi (¼ pint) double cream

Crush the biscuits finely and sprinkle the crumbs in the bottom of a buttered 23-cm (9-in) loose-bottomed cake tin.

Beat the cottage cheese until smooth. Add the milk, cornflour and egg yolks and beat well together. Whisk the egg whites stiffly and fold into the mixture with the sugar and lemon juice. Pour into the cake tin. Bake in the oven for 30–35 minutes at 180°C (350°F) mark 4 until well risen and firm to the touch. Leave to cool.

Whisk the cream until stiff. Carefully remove the cake from the tin and pipe or spoon the cream around the top to decorate.
Serves 6

To **freeze** Open freeze, then wrap in foil or pack into a rigid container. To serve, unwrap and thaw in the refrigerator overnight.

DINNER PARTY FOR 6

Tarte à l'oignon	Haddock and prawn mousse	Chocolate plum chiffon pie
	Tomato and courgette salad	
	New potato salad	

Tarte à l'oignon

700 g (1½ lb) onions, skinned
50 g (2 oz) butter
3 eggs
150 ml (¼ pint) milk
150 ml (¼ pint) single cream
salt and freshly ground pepper
grated nutmeg

For the pastry
100 g (4 oz) flour
40 g (1½ oz) butter
1 egg

Thinly slice the onions. Melt the butter in a large frying pan. Add the onions and fry gently, covered, for 20 minutes.

Meanwhile make the pastry. Sift together the flour and a pinch of salt, then mix in the remaining butter until it resembles fine bread-crumbs. Add the egg and enough cold water to form a dough. Knead lightly on a floured surface, then roll out and use to line a 20.5-cm (8-in) flan ring. Chill for 15 minutes.

Blend together the eggs, milk, cream and seasoning until smooth. Pour a little of the egg

mixture into the pastry case. Add the onions and the remaining egg mixture. Bake in the oven at 200°C (400°F) mark 6 for 30 minutes until golden brown and set. Serve hot or cold.
Serves 6

To freeze Cool quickly, then wrap in foil. To serve, unwrap and thaw at room temperature for 4 hours. To serve hot, thaw as above and reheat in the oven at 180°C (350°F) mark 4 for 25–30 minutes.

Haddock and prawn mousse

1 medium onion, skinned
450 g (1 lb) haddock fillets, skinned
1 bay leaf
300 ml (½ pint) milk
salt and freshly ground pepper
25 g (1 oz) butter
25 g (1 oz) flour
1 egg, separated
few drops of anchovy essence
15 g (½ oz) powdered gelatine
150 ml (¼ pint) mayonnaise (see page 63)
150 ml (¼ pint) single cream
225 g (8 oz) frozen prawns, thawed
cucumber slices

Roughly chop the onion and place in a sauce-pan with the fish, bay leaf, milk and season-ing. Poach for 15 minutes until tender. Strain the liquid and make up to 300 ml (½ pint) with water. Discard the bay leaf.

Blend together the butter, flour and fish liquid. Pour into a saucepan and bring to the boil, whisking, to thicken. Blend the fish with the egg yolk to form a purée and stir into the sauce with the anchovy essence. Dissolve the gelatine

106

in 30 ml (2 tbsp) water in a small bowl over a pan of boiling water. Add the gelatine to the fish mixture and cool. Stir in the mayonnaise and cream. Stiffly whisk the egg white and fold into the mixture. Decorate the base of a 22-cm (8½-in) spring-release cake tin with a few whole prawns and cucumber slices. Roughly chop the remaining prawns and fold into the fish mixture. Spoon into the tin and chill until set. Unmould to serve.
Serves 6

Not suitable for freezing

Tomato courgette salad

450 g (1 lb) firm ripe tomatoes, skinned
450 g (1 lb) courgettes, washed
105 ml (7 tbsp) vegetable oil
15 ml (1 tbsp) chopped fresh chives
30 ml (2 tbsp) tarragon vinegar
salt and freshly ground pepper

Roughly chop the tomatoes. Thickly slice the courgettes. Heat 45 ml (3 tbsp) oil in a large frying pan and sauté the courgettes until golden brown. Put the courgettes and tomatoes in a serving dish. Blend together the chives, vinegar, seasoning and remaining oil. Pour the dressing over the salad and toss. Chill before serving.
Serves 6

Not suitable for freezing

New potato salad

700 g (1½ lb) small new potatoes, scrubbed
½ bunch spring onions, washed and trimmed
90 ml (6 tbsp) vegetable oil
30 ml (2 tbsp) wine vinegar
2.5 ml (½ level tsp) French mustard
salt and freshly ground pepper
60 ml (4 tbsp) single cream
chopped fresh parsley to garnish

Cook the potatoes in boiling salted water for 15–20 minutes until tender, then drain thoroughly. Roughly chop the onions and add to the potatoes. Blend together the oil, vinegar, mustard and seasoning and pour over the potatoes while still warm. Cover and leave to cool. Before serving, stir in the cream, spoon into a serving dish and sprinkle with parsley.
Serves 6

Not suitable for freezing

Chocolate plum chiffon pie

75 g (3 oz) butter
225 g (8 oz) chocolate digestive biscuits
15 g (½ oz) gelatine
553-g (1lb 3½-oz) can red plums, stoned
225 g (8 oz) curd cheese
150 ml (¼ pint) soured cream
grated rind and juice of 1 orange
30 ml (2 tbsp) lemon juice
2 egg whites
grated chocolate to decorate

Melt the butter in a saucepan. Crush the biscuits and stir well into the butter. Press into a 23-cm (9-in) loose-bottomed cake tin. Sprinkle the gelatine into 45 ml (3 tbsp) water in a small bowl. Stand over a saucepan of boiling water and stir until dissolved. Leave to cool.

Blend the plums and syrup together to form a purée. Beat in the cheese, soured cream, orange rind and juice and lemon juice.

Whisk the egg whites until stiff and fold the cooled gelatine and then the egg whites into the plum mixture. Pour over the biscuit base and leave in the refrigerator to set. Remove from the tin and sprinkle the top with grated chocolate. Serve chilled.
Serves 6

To freeze When set, open freeze and wrap with foil. To serve, thaw at room temperature for about 3 hours.

BUFFET TO SERVE WITH DRINKS FOR 8

Cheese olives	Savoury choux puffs
Spicy cheese bobs	Sardine pyramids
Prawn bites	Asparagus chicken quiches

Cheese olives

225 g (8 oz) cream cheese
15 ml (1 tbsp) chopped fresh parsley
15 stuffed olives
50 g (2 oz) shelled walnuts

Blend the cheese and parsley until smooth. Roll small amounts of cheese around each olive to enclose completely. Chop the walnuts finely and toss the olives in the nuts. Chill for an hour. Cut in half with a sharp knife before serving.
Makes 30 halves

Not suitable for freezing

Spicy cheese bobs

225 g (8 oz) Cheddar cheese
60 ml (4 level tbsp) mango chutney
5 ml (1 level tsp) curry powder
100 g (4 oz) whole blanched almonds

Finely grate the cheese. Blend together with the chutney and curry powder to a firm paste. Roll small quantities of the cheese paste around half the almonds. Finely chop the remaining nuts and press the chopped nuts into the cheese.
Makes 24

Not suitable for freezing

Prawn bites

100 g (4 oz) plain flour
pinch of salt
25 g (1 oz) lard
150 g (5 oz) butter
50 g (2 oz) Cheddar cheese
beaten egg
184-g (6-oz) can prawns, drained
2.5 ml ($\frac{1}{2}$ level tsp) tomato purée

Sift together the flour and salt. Mix in the lard and 25 g (1 oz) butter until it resembles fine breadcrumbs. Grate the cheese and add with enough cold water to form a soft dough. Roll out the pastry on a lightly floured surface to form a 20.5 × 30.5-cm (8 × 12-in) rectangle. Trim the edges and mark into 2.5 × 5-cm (1 × 2-in) strips. Brush with beaten egg, place on a baking tray and bake in the oven at 200°C (400°F) mark 6 for 15 minutes until golden. Cool on a wire rack.

Blend together half the prawns, the remaining butter and the tomato purée until smooth. Using a star vegetable nozzle pipe lines of the shrimp butter on to the cheese bases. Garnish with the remaining whole prawns.
Makes 48

To freeze Cool the baked pastry rectangles, then wrap. Pack the prawn mixture into a rigid container. To serve, thaw both at room temperature for 3 hours and finish as above.

Savoury choux puffs

50 g (2 oz) margarine
65 g (2½ oz) plain flour
2 eggs, beaten
100 g (4 oz) cream cheese
50 g (2 oz) butter
5 ml (1 tsp) lemon juice
pinch of garlic salt

Melt the margarine in 150 ml (¼ pint) water. Remove from the heat and beat in the flour. Cool slightly. Mix in the eggs gradually, beating well to form a piping consistency.

Using a 1-cm (½-in) plain vegetable nozzle, pipe 24 small walnut-sized balls of paste on to a baking sheet. Bake in the oven at 200°C (400°F) mark 6 for 15–20 minutes until well risen, golden and crisp. Make a slit in the side of each to let out the steam and cool on a wire rack.

Blend together the cheese, butter, lemon juice and garlic salt. Using a very small plain vegetable nozzle, pipe the filling into the puffs.
Makes 24

To freeze Cool the unfilled puffs then pack into a rigid container and freeze. To serve, thaw unwrapped at room temperature for 1 hour. Crisp in the oven at 180°C (350°F) mark 4 for 4–5 minutes, then cool and fill as above.

Sardine pyramids

24 cocktail rusk biscuits
butter
two 125-g (4⅜-oz) cans sardines, drained
15 ml (1 tbsp) lemon juice
salt and freshly ground pepper
paprika or chopped fresh parsley to garnish

Lightly spread the biscuits with butter. Blend together the sardines, lemon juice and seasoning until smooth. Mound small spoonfuls of the mixture on the biscuits. Using a damp skewer dipped in the paprika or parsley mark a cross on top of each.
Makes 24

Not suitable for freezing

Asparagus chicken quiches

175 g (6 oz) shortcrust pastry (see page 57)
75 g (3 oz) cooked asparagus stalks
100 g (4 oz) cooked chicken
50 g (2 oz) Stilton cheese, crumbled
50 ml (2 fl oz) milk
1 egg, beaten
freshly ground black pepper
watercress to garnish

Roll out the pastry and use to line four 9-cm (3½-in) individual round Yorkshire pudding tins. Roughly chop the asparagus and chicken and mix together. Spoon into the pastry cases and sprinkle over the cheese.

Beat together the milk, egg and seasoning and pour into the flan cases. Bake the quiches in the oven at 190°C (375°F) mark 5 for 30 minutes until the filling is set and light golden brown. Cut into quarters, garnish with watercress and serve hot or cold.
Makes 16

To freeze When cold, pack into a rigid container. To serve cold, leave to thaw, covered, at room temperature for 4 hours. To serve hot, replace the frozen flans in tins or on a baking tray and reheat in the oven at 180°C (350°F) mark 4 for 30 minutes or until warmed through.

Tuna fish creams	Spaghetti provençal	Apple and orange vacherin
	Puff top turkey pie	
	Red cabbage slaw	
	Marinated mushroom salad	

Tuna fish creams

$\frac{1}{2}$ a small onion, skinned
15 ml (1 level tbsp) capers
450 ml ($\frac{3}{4}$ pint) soured cream
60 ml (4 level tbsp) mayonnaise (see page 63)
salt and freshly ground pepper
dash of Worcestershire sauce
15 ml (1 tbsp) chopped fresh chives
15 g ($\frac{1}{2}$ oz) powdered gelatine
4 hard-boiled eggs
two 198-g (7-oz) cans tuna fish, drained
    and flaked
tomato wedges and parsley to garnish

Finely chop the onion and capers and blend together with the soured cream, mayonnaise, seasoning, Worcestershire sauce and chives. Dissolve the gelatine in 60 ml (4 tbsp) water in a small basin over a pan of hot water. Cool slightly, then stir into the cream mixture. Chop the eggs and add to the cream mixture with the fish. Spoon into one large or twelve individual soufflé dishes. Chill until set and garnish with the tomato and parsley.
Serves 12

Not suitable for freezing

> *Organise the way you use your food processor so that you do as little washing up as possible—for example mix pastry before you chop the vegetables and finish by chopping onions or meat.*

Spaghetti provençal

3 medium onions, skinned
2 garlic cloves, skinned
30 ml (2 tbsp) vegetable oil
1.4 kg (3 lb) boned shoulder of lamb
75 ml (5 level tbsp) flour
60 ml (4 level tbsp) tomato purée
30 ml (2 tbsp) fresh rosemary
pinch of nutmeg
450 g (1 lb) tomatoes, skinned and seeded
90 ml (6 tbsp) white wine
1.1 litre (2 pints) chicken or beef stock
salt and pepper
1 kg ($2\frac{1}{4}$ lbs) spaghetti
50 g (2 oz) butter
grated Parmesan cheese to serve

Slice the onions thinly and finely chop the garlic. Heat the oil in a large saucepan. Fry the onions and garlic for 10 minutes. Meanwhile mince the lamb and add to the onions. Fry, stirring, for 5 minutes. Stir in the flour and cook for 1 minute. Add the tomato purée, rosemary and nutmeg. Roughly chop the tomatoes and stir into the lamb mixture with the wine, stock and seasoning. Cover and simmer for $1\frac{1}{2}$ hours until the liquid is reduced by half and the meat tender.

Cook the spaghetti in boiling salted water for 20 minutes. Drain well, return to the pan, add the butter and toss until butter has melted. Turn into a large warm serving dish and pour the lamb on top. Sprinkle with Parmesan.
Serves 12

To freeze Cool the lamb sauce quickly and pack into a rigid container. To serve, place the frozen sauce in a large saucepan and heat gently, stirring, until hot. Cook the spaghetti and serve as above.

Puff top turkey pie

3.2-kg (7-lb) oven-ready turkey
onion, carrot, bay leaves and peppercorns
for flavouring
900 g (2 lb) leeks, trimmed
225 g (8 oz) butter or margarine
275 g (10 oz) flour
150 ml ($\frac{1}{4}$ pint) dry white wine
salt and freshly ground pepper
225 g (8 oz) Cheddar cheese
4 eggs, beaten

Place the turkey in a large saucepan. Add the flavouring ingredients and cover with water. Bring to the boil, then simmer for $1\frac{1}{2}$ hours until tender. Remove the bird and strain and reserve the liquid. Remove the flesh and chop roughly, discarding any skin and bones. Slice the leeks thinly and wash well. Blanch in boiling water for 2 minutes and drain thoroughly. Place the turkey and leeks in two 2.3-litre (4-pint) shallow ovenproof casseroles or dishes.

Blend together 100 g (4 oz) fat and 100 g (4 oz) flour with 1 litre ($1\frac{3}{4}$ pints) of the reserved turkey stock and the wine and seasoning. Pour into a saucepan and bring to the boil, whisking to thicken. Pour the sauce over the turkey and leeks.

Melt the remaining fat in 300 ml ($\frac{1}{2}$ pint) water. Bring to the boil, remove from the heat and beat in the flour. Cool slightly. Grate the cheese. Gradually beat the eggs into the flour mixture with 200 g (7 oz) of the cheese, keeping the mixture stiff. Place large spoonfuls on top of the turkey. Sprinkle over the remaining cheese and bake at once in the oven at 220°C (425°F) mark 7 for about 40 minutes until golden brown.
Serves 12

To freeze Cool the turkey and sauce mixture and pack into a rigid container. To serve, thaw overnight in a refrigerator, spoon into oven proof dishes and make the topping for the pie as above.

Red cabbage slaw

900 g (2 lb) red cabbage
450 g (1 lb) carrots, peeled
450 g (1 lb) red-skinned eating apples,
quartered and cored
100 g (4 oz) seedless raisins
150 ml ($\frac{1}{4}$ pint) vegetable oil
75 ml (5 tbsp) white wine vinegar
30 ml (2 level tbsp) made mustard
salt and freshly ground pepper
chopped fresh parsley to garnish

Remove the outer leaves and hard core from the cabbage and shred finely. Grate the carrots and slice the apples. Mix together with the raisins.

Blend together the oil, vinegar, mustard and seasoning. Pour over the salad and toss well. Cover tightly and chill in the refrigerator for 2 hours. Toss again, spoon into a serving dish and sprinkle with parsley.
Serves 12

Not suitable for freezing

Marinated mushroom salad

700 g ($1\frac{1}{2}$ lb) button mushrooms, wiped
350 g (12 oz) celery, washed
350 g (12 oz) onion, skinned
90 ml (6 tbsp) chopped fresh parsley
225 ml (8 fl oz) vegetable oil
200 ml (7 fl oz) red wine vinegar
30 ml (2 level tbsp) dark brown sugar
30 ml (2 level tbsp) tomato purée
salt and freshly ground pepper

Slice the mushrooms, celery and onion. Mix together in a bowl with the parsley. Blend together the remaining ingredients and pour over the salad. Toss well, cover and leave to marinate in a refrigerator for 3 hours. Spoon into a serving dish.
Serves 12

Not suitable for freezing

Apple and orange vacherin

6 egg whites
350 g (12 oz) caster sugar
1.4 kg (3 lb) cooking apples
75 g (3 oz) granulated sugar
3 medium oranges
300 ml ($\frac{1}{2}$ pint) whipping cream
icing sugar to decorate

Line two baking trays with non-stick paper. Whisk the egg whites very stiffly, add half the sugar and whisk again. Fold in the remaining sugar. Spread or pipe four 15-cm (6-in) rounds on the baking trays. Dry out in the oven at 100°C (200°F) mark $\frac{1}{2}$ for about 2 hours. Cool on wire racks and peel off the paper.

Peel, quarter, core and slice the apples. Place in a large saucepan. Add the granulated sugar, finely grated rind of the oranges and 90 ml (6 tbsp) water. Cover the pan and cook gently until the apples are soft but retain their shape. Remove the skin and pith remaining on the oranges and divide the orange flesh into segments. Stir into the apple mixture.

Place two meringue rounds on flat plates and divide the apple mixture between them. Whip the cream until stiff and spread over the apple. Top with the remaining meringue rounds, dust with sifted icing sugar and serve.
Serves 12

To freeze Open freeze the rounds of meringue and pack into a rigid container. Cool the apple and orange mixture and pack into a rigid container. To serve, thaw the meringue rounds and apple filling at room temperature for 3 hours and fill as above.

CHILDREN'S PARTY FOR 10

Tuna cheese balls
Chicken puffs
Nutty sausage fingers
Cheese salad
Mandarin flake flan
Chocolate mousse

Tuna cheese balls

1 stick of celery, washed
198-g (7-oz) can tuna fish, drained
100 g (4 oz) cream cheese
salt and freshly ground pepper
grated rind and juice of $\frac{1}{2}$ a lemon
25 g (1 oz) cheese and onion crisps

Chop the celery finely. Beat the celery, tuna, cheese, seasoning, lemon rind and juice well together. Cover and leave in the refrigerator to chill. When firm, roll into 20 balls. Crush the crisps and use to coat the balls.
Makes 20

To freeze Before coating with the crisps, pack in a rigid container with greaseproof paper between the layers. To serve, allow to thaw in refrigerator for about 4 hours, then coat with crisps.

> *Use your food processor or blender to blend all the ingredients for white or other roux-based sauces, then simply bring the mixture to the boil.*

Chicken puffs

450 g (1 lb) cooked chicken
1 medium onion, skinned
50 g (2 oz) butter
50 g (2 oz) flour
300 ml ($\frac{1}{2}$ pint) milk
salt and freshly ground pepper
juice of $\frac{1}{2}$ a lemon
369-g (13-oz) packet frozen puff pastry, thawed
1 egg, beaten

Roughly chop the chicken. Chop the onion finely. Melt half the butter in a saucepan and fry the onion for 10 minutes. Blend the remaining butter, flour, milk and seasoning together until smooth. Pour into the saucepan with the onion and bring to the boil, whisking until thick. Cook for 1–2 minutes. Add the chicken and lemon juice. Cover with damp greaseproof and leave to cool.

Roll out the pastry and cut out twenty 10-cm (4-in) rounds. Divide the chicken mixture between the rounds. Brush the edges with egg, fold in half and seal the edges well. Place on a baking tray and bake in the oven at 200°C (400°F) mark 6 for 15–20 minutes until well risen and golden. Cool on a wire rack.
Makes 20

To freeze When cool, pack into a rigid container. To serve, thaw at room temperature for 3–4 hours.

Nutty sausage fingers

175 g (6 oz) shortcrust pastry
   (see page 57)
10 ml (2 level tsp) yeast extract
1 small apple, peeled and cored
1 stick of celery
225 g (8 oz) pork sausagemeat
15 ml (1 level tbsp) sweet chutney
15 ml (1 level tbsp) tomato purée
salt and freshly ground pepper
25 g (1 oz) salted peanuts
40 g (1½ oz) cheese
25 g (1 oz) fresh white breadcrumbs

Roll out the pastry to a rectangle 30.5 × 12.5 cm (12 × 5 in). Place on a lightly floured baking sheet and spread yeast extract evenly over the pastry. Finely chop the apple and celery and mix with the sausagemeat, chutney, tomato purée and seasoning. Spread over the pastry. Roughly chop the peanuts and grate the cheese. Mix with the breadcrumbs and sprinkle over the sausage mixture.

Bake in the oven at 190°C (375°F) mark 5 for 30 minutes until crisp and golden brown. Leave to cool on the baking sheet, then cut into 10 fingers and cut in half lengthways.
Makes 20

To freeze Open freeze, then pack in a rigid container. To serve, thaw at room temperature for 4 hours. Put under a hot grill for 2 minutes to crisp the topping.

Cheese salad

450 g (1 lb) white cabbage
1 large carrot, peeled
1 large red-skinned eating apple,
   quartered and cored
45 ml (3 level tbsp) mayonnaise (see page 63)
45 ml (3 level tbsp) soured cream
grated rind and juice of ½ a lemon
salt and freshly ground pepper
275 g (10 oz) Red Leicester cheese
chopped fresh parsley to garnish

Shred the cabbage finely. Grate the carrot and slice the apple. Place in a bowl with the mayonnaise, soured cream, lemon rind and juice and seasoning. Cube the cheese, add to the salad and toss well. Spoon into a serving dish and sprinkle with parsley.
Serves 10

Not suitable for freezing

Mandarin flake flan

75 g (3 oz) butter
90 g (3½ oz) sugar
15 ml (1 heaped tbsp) golden syrup
100 g (4 oz) cornflakes
2 packets orange jelly
2 eggs, separated
300 ml (½ pint) milk
grated rind and juice of 1 large orange
550 g (1¼ lb) cottage cheese
15 g (½ oz) caster sugar
150 ml (¼ pint) whipping cream
298-g (10½-oz) can mandarin oranges,
   drained

Melt the butter, 75 g (3 oz) sugar and syrup together in a saucepan. Stir in the cornflakes until evenly coated. Spoon into a 28-cm (11-in) spring-clip cake tin and press over the bottom.

Place the jelly and 60 ml (4 tbsp) water in a small saucepan and heat gently, stirring until dissolved. Allow to cool slightly. Beat together the egg yolks and milk. Pour on to the jelly, stir and heat for a few minutes without boiling.

Remove the jelly mixture from the heat and add the orange rind and juice. Stir in the cottage cheese. Whisk the egg whites until stiff and fold in the remaining sugar. Whisk the cream until stiff and fold into the cheese mixture with the egg whites. Pour over the cornflakes and put in the refrigerator to chill and set. Decorate with mandarin segments.
Serves 10

Not suitable for freezing

Chocolate mousse

450 g (1 lb) plain chocolate
8 eggs, separated
30 ml (2 tbsp) orange juice
25 g (1 oz) butter
hundreds and thousands, chocolate
**   vermicelli, glacé cherries or**
**   flaked almonds to decorate**

Break up the chocolate and put in a basin over a pan of hot water until melted. Remove from the heat and mix in the egg yolks, one at a time, the orange juice and the butter. Leave to cool. Whisk the egg whites until stiff and fold them into the chocolate mixture until thoroughly mixed. Spoon into 10 small dishes and decorate.
Serves 10

To freeze Cover the dishes with foil, omitting the decoration. To serve, thaw in the refrigerator for 2–3 hours and serve chilled, decorated as above.

Hungarian liver sausage ramekins	Tenderloin casserole	French apple flan
	Sliced jacket potatoes	
	Parsnip and carrot au gratin	

Hungarian liver sausage ramekins

175 g (6 oz) liver sausage
2 hard-boiled eggs
salt and freshly ground pepper
1 garlic clove, skinned
15 ml (1 tbsp) chopped fresh mixed herbs
60 ml (4 tbsp) soured cream
1 medium gherkin
1 small onion, skinned
parsley sprigs to garnish
French bread

Blend together the liver sausage, eggs, seasoning, garlic, herbs and soured cream until smooth. Finely chop the gherkin and onion and stir into the mixture. Spoon into four small ramekin dishes and smooth the top. Chill for 1–2 hours in the refrigerator. Garnish with parsley and serve with hot crusty French bread.
Serves 4

To freeze Cover the dishes with foil, omitting the garnish. To serve, thaw in the refrigerator overnight and garnish as above.

> *Use your hand mixer over the cooker to remove lumps from sauces and take the effort out of making really smooth mashed potatoes.*

Tenderloin casserole

Illustrated in colour facing page 96

700 g (1½ lb) pork tenderloin
30 ml (2 tbsp) vegetable oil
25 g (1 oz) butter
2 large onions, skinned
1 garlic clove, skinned
225 g (8 oz) tomatoes, skinned
30 ml (2 level tbsp) plain flour
300 ml (½ pint) dry white wine
15 ml (1 level tbsp) tomato purée
salt and freshly ground pepper
1 medium green pepper
1 medium red pepper
10 black olives, stoned

Remove any skin and fat then cube the pork. Heat the oil and butter in a large flameproof casserole and fry the meat for 5–10 minutes until brown. Remove from the pan. Slice the onions finely. Finely chop the garlic. Fry the onions and garlic for 10 minutes until golden. Chop the tomatoes and stir into the onions with the flour, wine, tomato purée and seasoning. Bring to the boil, stirring, and add the meat.

Cover and cook in the oven at 180°C (350°F) mark 4 for about 50 minutes. Slice the peppers thinly, add to the casserole with the olives and cook for a further 20 minutes.
Serves 4

To freeze Cool quickly, then cover the dish or pack into a rigid container, omitting the parsley. To serve, reheat the frozen pork, covered, in the oven at 180°C (350°F) mark 4 for 1–1½ hours until heated through.

Sliced jacket potatoes

Illustrated in colour facing page 96

900 g (2 lb) medium potatoes
50 g (2 oz) butter
salt and freshly ground pepper
60 ml (4 tbsp) chopped fresh parsley

Scrub but do not peel the potatoes. Boil until just tender, then slice thickly. Arrange the slices overlapping in an ovenproof serving dish. Melt the butter and add the seasoning and parsley. Pour the butter over the potatoes and cover and keep warm until required.
Serves 4

Not suitable for freezing

Parsnip and carrot au gratin

Illustrated in colour facing page 96

450 g (1 lb) parsnips, peeled
450 g (1 lb) carrots, peeled
600 ml (1 pint) chicken stock
salt and freshly ground pepper
25 g (1 oz) butter, melted
50 g (2 oz) fresh breadcrumbs
chopped fresh parsley

Slice the parsnips and carrots thinly. Place in a saucepan with the stock and seasoning. Bring to the boil, cover and simmer gently for 20 minutes until tender. Drain and spoon the vegetables into a warm flameproof dish. Pour over the butter and sprinkle with breadcrumbs and parsley. Place under a hot grill until golden brown.
Serves 4

Not suitable for freezing

French apple flan

50 g (2 oz) plain flour
50 g (2 oz) self raising flour
50 g (2 oz) butter
25 g (1 oz) icing sugar
6 red-skinned eating apples
15–30 ml (1–2 level tbsp) caster sugar
juice of 1 lemon
30 ml (2 level tbsp) apricot jam
whipping cream

Sift the flours together and mix in the butter until it resembles fine breadcrumbs. Add the icing sugar and enough cold water to form a soft dough. Roll out on a floured surface to line a 20.5-cm (8-in) flan ring.

Peel, core and chop four apples. Place in a saucepan with 30 ml (2 tbsp) water, the sugar and half the lemon juice and cook gently for about 15 minutes until pulpy. Blend to form a smooth purée. Spoon over the bottom of the flan case. Core and slice the remaining apples and dip in the remaining lemon juice.

Arrange the apple slices over the apple purée. Bake in the oven at 200°C (400°F) mark 6 for about 25–30 minutes. Melt the apricot jam in 15 ml (1 tbsp) water. Sieve into a bowl and brush over the apple slices while still warm. Serve warm or cold, with cream.
Serves 4

To freeze Cool, open freeze then wrap. To serve, unwrap and thaw at room temperature for 4 hours.

Glossary

Bake blind   To bake flan cases, tarts and tartlet pastry cases without a filling. The pastry may be lined with greaseproof paper and dried beans, foil, or small tartlet cases may just be pricked with a fork.

Blanch   To treat food with boiling water in order to whiten it; to preserve its natural colour; to loosen its skin; to remove any strong or bitter taste; to kill unwanted enzymes before freezing or preserving.

Croûtons   Small pieces of bread which are fried or toasted and served as an accompaniment to soup or as a garnish.

Knock up   To make horizontal cuts with the back of a knife blade in the sealed pastry edges of a covered or double-crust pie before baking.

Sauté   To fry lightly in a little butter and/or oil, sometimes adding a little stock towards the end of cooking. A sauté pan has a wide base which allows plenty of room. Alternatively, use a frying pan with a lid.

Scallop   To decorate the double edge of the pastry covering of a pie. Traditionally the scallop for sweet dishes should be small and for savoury pies wider apart.

Setting point   Test the set of jelly or jam after a spoonful has been left to cool on a saucer. If the jelly wrinkles when the little finger is drawn through it, it is ready for pouring into pots for setting.

Index